BOOT CAMP THERAPY

BOOT CAMP THERAPY

Brief, Action-Oriented Clinical
Approaches to Anger, Anxiety,
and Depression

ROBERT TAIBBI

W. W. NORTON & COMPANY
New York • London

For information about permission to reproduce selections from this book, write to Permissions, W. W. Norton & Company, Inc., 500 Fifth Avenue, New York, NY 10110

For information about special discounts for bulk purchases, please contact W. W. Norton Special Sales at specialsales@wwnorton.com or 800-233-4830

Manufacturing by Quad Graphics Fairfield
Book design by Gilda Hannah
Production manager: Leeann Graham

Library of Congress Cataloging-in-Publication Data

Taibbi, Robert.
   Boot camp therapy: brief, action-oriented clinical approaches to anxiety, anger, & depression / Robert Taibbi. — First edition.
        pages cm
"A Norton professional book."
Includes bibliographical references and index.
ISBN 978-0-393-70823-3 (hardcover)
1. Brief psychotherapy. 2. Anxiety—Treatment. 3. Anger—Treatment. 4. Depression, Mental—Treatment. I. Title.
   RC480.55.T338 2014
   616.89'147—dc23
                                    2013012775

ISBN: 978-0-393-70823-3

W. W. Norton & Company, Inc., 500 Fifth Avenue, New York, N.Y. 10110
                        www.wwnorton.com
W. W. Norton & Company Ltd., Castle House, 75/76 Wells Street, London
W1T 3QT

1 2 3 4 5 6 7 8 9 0

Contents

CHAPTER ONE

Brief Therapy Meets Boot Camp

"I DON'T KNOW WHY I'M HERE," says Jack. *"My older son and I got into it the other night. Well, my wife got scared and called the police. They charged me with assault. Sure, I was upset but that was because my son has no right to disrespect me."*

"I guess I'm here because I'm anxious all the time." Tamara is sitting at the edge of her seat and there is a slight tremor in her hands as she talks. *"I had a panic attack last year, out of the blue. I never had one before or since, but I've been nervous. I've always been nervous. Little things like worrying about being late for an appointment—I was worried that I was going to be late coming here—or imagining bad things happening, or when I'm with a group of people that I'm going to say the wrong thing."*

"I've been on and off depressed most of my life," says Ann. *"I know it runs in my family. My father struggled with it as far back as I can remember. But I've always been able to get over it somehow. But these last 6 months, since they started doing layoffs at my job, I can't. I'm having trouble sleeping. The morale at work is awful. I dread going in. I'd quit if I could afford it, but at my age no one is going to hire me. I feel trapped."*

We can imagine clients like Jack, Tamara, and Ann sitting in mental health centers, clinics, and private practice offices all across the country. There are clients like Jack, who may be ordered by the court for anger management, or who are abusive in their marriages, or who bully other students at school; there are others like Tamara, with panic attacks and generalized anxiety, or its cousins posttraumatic stress disorder (PTSD) and obsessive-compulsive disorder (OCD), affecting 40 million Americans (Kessler, Chiu, Demler, & Walters, 2005); and there are yet others like Ann, with situational depression, the grief of loss, the chronic undertow of dysthymia, or the immobilizing despair of major depression. Such clients come in because someone tells them to or because they no longer can cope on their own, because they are seeking relief. Unfortunately, however, whatever drives them in, they're not likely to stay very long.

The World of Brief

The images of therapy as a long-term process persist in our cultural psyche. The analyst's couch; the notion of years of unraveling, exploring, and tramping through childhood; and Woody Allen movies and *Mad Men* help keep these impressions alive. But the reality is much different, and the research tells another story: Clients come for an average of 5–8 sessions (Cooper, 2011; Phillips, 1985), most come only once (Phillips, 1985), and 70% drop out before reaching their goals (Garfield, 1986).

So while we may like to believe otherwise, most therapy is, by default, if not always by design, brief. Surely, some sources of these statistics reflect the mismatched expectations of clinician and client. At one point during my years of working in community mental health, my colleagues and I decided to survey new clients about their expectations. Most, we discovered, had never been in any type of counseling or therapy previously; most were looking for a therapist who was "nice," who would "offer advice," and who would "listen"; most thought they would need to come no more than 1–2 times. And when you think about it, this made sense. What they expected was a process akin to that of seeing the family doctor—walk in, state the problem and the symptoms, get a diagnosis, walk out with a prescription, and maybe, just maybe, go back for a follow-up appointment.

Imagine these clients' dismay when in the first session they invariably spent half the time doing intake, going through page after page of seemingly trivial questions (Social Security numbers, children's birthdates), sign here, here, and here—finally seeing a therapist for a few minutes before hearing, "Well, it looks like we're about out of time for today. Thanks so much for coming in. Let's continue this next week at the same time." It's easy to imagine such clients walking out shaking their heads and saying, "Continue what? I wasn't told anything." Perhaps they'll come back, but if they do, the research tells us that they'd better leave this time with some guidance.

All this expectation of results is undoubtedly now further intensified by our technologically fueled need for instant gratification. The image of the rarely speaking analyst is rapidly being displaced by a Dr. Phil who every day is able to drill down and offer his assessment and advice to television clients in a half hour, more closely mimicking in the minds of his viewers what they see their family doctor do at every visit. In Dr. Phil's corner we can find the insurance companies and managed care process, limiting what clients can and cannot receive (for example, a limit of 10 sessions in a year, the need to refer for antidepressant medication, absolutely no couples therapy), shaping or reshaping not only our therapeutic style but also, indelibly, our clients' notions of what should or can happen.

Finally, the biggest log on the fire has to be financial pressures, leaving clients wincing every time they write their copay check and leaving the public sector—the community clinics and counseling services on college campuses—grimacing each month as they stare at their overall budgets. Budget cuts mean fewer staff, longer waiting lists, the need to quickly move clients on, and the requirement to limit the number of sessions that can be offered so that more clients can potentially be served. The slow building of rapport and that several-session assessment before introducing a treatment plan have for most therapists and clients alike gone the way of the analyst's couch. Brief is here.

Brief as Old

Brief therapy is popular today but it has been here a long time. Even our impression of Freud and the psychoanalytic process is skewed. According to historians, not only was "Little Hans" a one-session wonder, but during Freud's early years his therapeutic work was typically much briefer than the stereotype. It was only when he introduced the free association technique later in life and his role became more passive that he felt uncomfortable working with so many clients and restricted his work to a long-term few (Messer & Warren, 1998).

Brief work hit its stride beginning in the 1980s in the solution-focused work of de Shazer (1985), Berg (1994), O'Hanlon (1999, 2006), and others, and it continues to this day. There are brief models of psychodynamic therapy (Messer & Warren, 1998), couples work (Halford, 2001), work with children (Berg & Steiner, 2003), treatment of severe mental illness (O'Hanlon & Weiner-Davis, 2003), and plenty of specifics on techniques and skills (Binder, 2010; Budman, Hoyt, & Friedman, 1992; Lipchik, 2002). Recently and not surprisingly, the principles of brief therapy have jumped the tracks into the field of life coaching (Szabo, Meier, & Pierolf, 2009). An always active, if not always major, player in the psychotherapy field, brief has in our current climate become invigorated.

The Core of Brief

So what makes brief *brief?* Our obvious first thought is time, or rather the limits on it. Some practitioners cap the number of sessions—10, for example—and then, ready or not, you're done; others are against rigid time frames. Some conceive of therapy as serial contact—pockets of brief work, with clients returning when new developmental crises arise (Budman, Hoyt, & Friedman, 1992); others stress "time used at maximum efficiency" (Binder, 2010). Brief, for these clinicians, becomes less "get it done" and more about the how and what you decide to get done. It becomes a way of thinking and looking at the therapeutic process that is different from the way a clinician committed to long-term work would see it.

Even with a quick glance at the brief therapy literature, we can easily discern the common elements that run through the various brief therapy approaches. Preston (1998), defines the central components of brief therapy and provides a good summary of what many brief clinicians would probably agree on:

Rapid assessment. While each clinician's theoretical foundation will obviously determine what he or she looks for and how he or she conceptualizes a client's presenting problem, there is a clear consensus that there's little to no room for gradual unfolding or deep pondering. Like family physicians, brief therapists start from the client's bundle of stated problems and symptoms, gather whatever additional information they need to connect it to their mental templates, and quickly assemble both an assessment and preliminary treatment plan from which to begin. And as with the physician, assessment and treatment usually go hand in hand: Try this, see what happens, and if nothing or only a little happens, we've learned something important that helps fine-tune our assessment and plan.

Specific focus/goals. Brief therapy is not about an extreme makeover; there is no overhaul or reconstruction of your personality or life. The focus is on the more narrow, "relevant" issues—what's most on your mind, what you need most to fix, what you most want to do or not do. And when that's done, we're done.

That being said, there is usually a broader, applicable takeaway. For some, it's information and a skill. The partners who engage in brief couples therapy undoubtedly learn how to listen and communicate better and, by continuing to apply these skills, will be able to avoid a host of problems in the future. The parents who quickly learn the value of structure and routine in managing their children can continue to do this as their children grow.

Similarly, clients can leave learning how to think more like a therapist. Systems-oriented family therapists are good at thinking in terms of patterns, rather than of people and pathology. Assessment becomes detecting the pattern; treatment concentrates on breaking it. Even after a brief stint of family therapy, with therapists talking about and pointing out patterns as they unfold in the room, clients quickly develop an eye for seeing them. With a successful therapy experience under their belts, clients can use these skills and often come to adapt themselves when dysfunctional patterns threaten to run amok.

Finally, as an additional by-product of their therapy experience, all clients gain their own impressions of the therapy process itself. For many brief therapy clients, what they walk away with is a sense that problems can be fixed relatively quickly, and they often see the experience as user friendly. This is what fuels the potential serial nature of brief therapy. Rather than do the major long-term excavation—exposing and reconstructing the foundation—we focus on the smaller projects: the leaky toilet, the failing air conditioner. If or when something else breaks, come on back.

Setting time limits. It could be argued that even the most long term of long-term therapists has an end point in mind. For the brief therapist the time is more specified and narrow: when the session limit is reached; when the presenting problem is resolved, at least for now; when the skills have been learned that the client can continue to apply—when Jack is less volatile with his son, when Tamara isn't obsessing all the time and is more functional in her everyday life, when Ann feels less depressed and less trapped at her job. When therapy relieves, reduces, or resolves the problem that the client initially walked in with, our job, for the time being, is done.

Targeted treatment strategies. Rapid assessment and specific goals require targeted strategies. Not carpet bombing, but rather, a surgical strike; not strip mining, but pinpoint drilling. The physician, to fight an infection, matches a specific drug with a specific virus. The brief therapist matches a specific problem with a specific course of treatment.

What the plan will be depends, as does the assessment, on the practitioner's theoretical foundation. The cognitive-behavioral assessment and subsequent treatment plan will be different from that which the systems-oriented or psychodynamic clinician might use. What they have in common is that the outcome is more an étude than a three-movement symphony.

Use of homework. If you are seeing clients four times a week for 4 years, there is little need for work outside the session. In such a micromanaged process, the session is the work itself. But if the sessions are limited in time and focus, much of the heavy lifting has to happen out there in the real world. Just as students who go to school for 2 hours a day are going to have a lot more homework to do at home than are those who have eight periods filled with study halls and time in class to complete it, the brief therapist needs to have clients go home and apply to their bigger world what is learned within a session.

Again, what this outside work entails varies with clinicians' orientation. But the notion that you actively apply what you discover and learn in a session is an essential aspect of brief therapy. This fits well with the focus on targeted treatment strategies, making change happen and then fine-tuning and regrouping.

Use of other sources of support. Within such a clinical approach and environment the therapist can't be *It.* If the work is narrowly defined and even intensively practiced, if much of it is out there in the real world, then it makes sense that real-world supports come into play. Students who have a teacher they can always go to—in class, in study hall—or parents to help with homework are different from students who are sent home with a heap of papers and assignments and left to muddle through on their own. This is perhaps where the family physician analogy breaks down. Clients can take their pills when necessary, but when their underlying problems include and affect others, it is the others whom we often need to share the load with. Brief therapy is often a group project. The group may be family and friends, Alcoholics Anonymous sponsors, members of support groups, or even correspondents online.

These criteria provide the framework for brief therapy. Is there something missing?

One topic not on the list is therapeutic rapport and the concomitant nuances of the clinician-client relationship. We know from research that how clients feel about us, as therapists, is more important than what we do (e.g., Lambert & Bailey, 2001). In longer-term therapies, rapport and trust have time to develop slowly, gradually wading into the therapeutic waters. While brief therapists obviously need to be empathic and sensitive, like the other aspects of brief therapy, rapport and trust need to be built quickly; the process is more of a plunge. While most clients seek out brief therapists because they are brief therapists, such therapists intentionally present themselves as confident and competent and proactively meet clients' expectations by letting them know at the onset about their own thinking and work patterns. By doing this, therapists avoid possible misunderstandings or spending large amounts of time negotiating or orienting clients to the clinical process.

But the other way that brief therapists build trust is through achieving results. By giving quick feedback about assessment and treatment, by using homework to produce behavioral change from the start, therapists foster in clients an awareness that the latter are in good hands. Just as trust in the competency of physicians increases when we discover that the medication they prescribed quickly alleviated our problem, so too will clients be able to relax and lean into the relationship when they find that what we recommend actually begins to make a difference.

This leads to another element of brief therapy not on Preston's (1998) list of criteria, namely, that strong leadership is clearly part and parcel of the brief therapy process. If the destination is clearly defined, and if the time is limited, you need a strong, clearheaded captain at the helm. Such a stance counters the frustration that many clients have of nondirective therapists—complaints that he didn't say much, that all she did was ask me how I felt. The brief therapist, in contrast, is more interactional and directive.

Finally, in brief therapists we find little talk about history and insight. Of course, this varies by the approach. While psychodynamic clinicians will still lean on these bulwarks of their model, most brief therapists are either ahistorical or use history sparingly as part of their assessment. Most brief work is about the present, where the power of therapeutic insight is replaced with the power of action, whether it is the breaking of patterns, learning new skills, or specifically altering thinking about situations, emotions, and problems in new ways.

The Boot Camp Approach

The Boot Camp approach has solidified in the past several years through a process of workshops being conducted nationally on various aspects of brief therapy. But actually the ideas represent the culmination of almost 40 years of clinical experience, primarily in community mental health. A majority of clients in these settings were often referred, had no prior experience with therapy, and didn't have the time, money, or inclination for long-term treatment. Most of all they looked at therapy as they would going to their family doctor. They were not interested in marching through the past or gaining insights but instead were looking for concrete steps they could be given so they could fix the problem that was currently on their mind. They were looking for a solution—be it "feeling better" after a few weeks of depression, "stopping getting so angry," or sorting out a specific marital or parenting issue.

Our approach follows in the footsteps of Preston's (1998) list. It is largely ahistorical, uses quick assessment, has a specific focus, assigns homework, uses results of homework to fine-tune the treatment plan, brings in outside family, friends, and others for support, and moves quickly to advance the changes. There is a decided emphasis, however, on several key elements:

Focus on immediate behavioral change. As the title and subtitle of this book suggest, this is an approach that hits the ground running. *Action oriented* here means behavioral change and *immediate* means as soon as the client leaves the office after the first appointment, if not before. While its core is based in systems theory and cognitive-behavioral therapy, behavior is the kingpin of change. As we will discuss further in Chapter 2, behavior, even more than thoughts, and certainly more than emotions, is the one thing that clients have the most control over and thus it can have the biggest impact on initiating change.

And research bears this out. In a 2006 study it was found that the behavioral components of a cognitive-behavioral approach were the most important elements in the treatment of depression (Dimidjian, Hollon, & Dobson, 2006). The mantra that we will be using throughout is, *If you keep doing the same thing, you keep feeling the same way.* Do it differently and your thoughts and emotions will catch up. The clinical issue isn't helping clients to feel or even think differently in order to act differently; we help them to act differently and their thinking and emotions will catch up. The treatment challenge is determining the size of the behavioral step and level of support clients need to successfully make these behavioral changes.

Focus on process. All forms of therapy focus on process, but in the Boot Camp approach this is the essential emphasis of both therapy sessions and treatment. Again, as we will be discussing further in Chapter 2, clients, by and large, and particularly those in crisis, tend to think in terms of content—what happened and when, the nature of symptoms, their theory, their story to explain how they feel, the stacking of facts and evidence to make their case.

In the Boot Camp approach, these facts and stories, even those in a client's history, are rarely important. The Boot Camp therapist is concerned with the *how* rather than the *what*: how clients approach problems, how they actively deal with troubling situations, emotions, or thoughts. Clinically the *how* obviously ties directly to clients' behaviors—helping them do things differently, taking action, focusing on process, using content, for example, to jump-start and motivate clients into taking risks and breaking patterns.

Detailed focus on process within those opening sessions is also vital, helping the therapist and client to hit the ground running and ensure success. This is the other mantra of the Boot Camp approach: *Track the process like a bloodhound.* What this means is that you need to make sure that you and the client are on the same page, that you are both working together as a team against the problem.

This is where many clinicians are lax—they fail to notice or they let it slide when a client is not engaged or seems ambivalent or when the client's verbal and nonverbal comments and commitments don't match. Good salespeople handle this well—they notice when customers hesitate, look away, raise an objection, say they'll think about it. Those successful in sales react, respond, tamp down that spark of doubt. And in that first session, and the one or two afterward, like it or not, we are salespeople trying to make the sale. We try to sell clients not only on us and our competence but also on our approach and its success. When we lose our focus, not only is valuable time lost, but both clinician and client become frustrated. The clinician easily begins to see a lack of motivation and resistance; the client sees and feels the mismatch between his or her own expectations and what the clinician is offering. When this happens the treatment never fully gets off the ground, or it stalls, or it is prematurely terminated.

So in describing how to implement the Boot Camp approach we will spend a lot of time tightening this focus and process, making sure the client is in lockstep with us as we move toward the agreed-on goal and path. At the slightest hint of wavering or disconnection, it is up to the clinician to notice and address what has just occurred. Do not pass go, do not move forward, but fix the problem in the room and in the relationship right then.

Focus on the core dynamic. The starting question for the Boot Camp therapist with any new client is "What keeps you from being able to solve this problem on your own?" If other people are able to handle these problems, or don't have them at all, why does this person struggle so? Often, as mentioned earlier, it is a matter of skill, what Ekstein and Wallerstein (1958) called "learning problems." A client struggles with money because she doesn't understand how to set up a budget; another struggles with parenting because he doesn't know that you can't manage a teenager the same way you approach an 8-year-old. In these cases, the beginning or often the entirety of treatment is helping these clients learn the skills they need. Once they do, they will be able to manage their money or parenting problems on their own in the future.

But more often than not, it is more than a matter of skill. This is what Ekstein referred to as "problems about learning." In these situations clients know the skills, but emotions override their ability to use them: "I know how to set up a budget, but when I feel depressed or angry at my partner, I go out and do shopping therapy"; "I basically am a good parent and know how to manage my teenager, but when I'm stressed and my daughter gives me that *look* I go ballistic and start World War III." The key to assessment for the Boot Camp therapist is figuring out what the client needs to learn most: the skill, the emotional override, or both.

But there is yet another layer to this, what in the Boot Camp approach is called the *core dynamic*. Emotional triggers—Ekstein's problems about learning—are often not simply about a client's immediate frustration with a partner or reaction to a daughter's facial expression but are both more generalized and deeper. Clients don't get stuck in their ability to solve superficial, isolated, or situational problems. Often their "stuckness," what gets them into trouble, is tied to their overall coping style and approach to problems.

And it is here that a brief therapist *does* get into history. What worked as a way of coping in the world as a child no longer works for the adult. The old software is outdated and inflexible. Clients who continue to use it are unable to effectively solve problems in the present-day, adult world, or they are left feeling continually rewounded and like a 10-year-old.

This is where the Boot Camp approach parts company with most brief therapies, and especially solution-focused approaches, and what makes it particularly unique. There is an *It* to be discovered: the way clients approach their problems and their coping style. If the therapist can quickly uncover this fatal flaw, and help clients respond in more flexible and adult ways not only to their presenting problem but in their overall approach to problems, they will walk away with a life-changing way of navigating their life.

No specific limits on sessions. This core dynamic can be assessed quickly. Once you've assessed it, your treatment plan, at least in your mind, is done. There may be skills to teach, behavioral assignments to titrate, supports to put in place, but the goal is clear. The essential step mentioned above is making certain that your vision and goals match those of the client. But once this is accomplished, you both are essentially done. Once clients are on board with this goal plan and know specifically what to focus on in their everyday life, the therapy is a matter of application, experience, and fine-tuning. Using the Boot Camp approach, clients often come in for 3–6 sessions, make clear behavioral steps toward their initial concerns, have a concrete plan for tackling the core dynamic, and then come in at varying intervals (weekly to biweekly to monthly) to maintain accountability and report or to fine-tune the initial treatment plan.

Again we can return to our physician example: If the underlying cause of a patient's presenting problem is largely one of lifestyle—diet, exercise, dealing with stress—the physician will provide acute care to get the patient stabilized and on board with the plan, determine what behaviors need to be changed and what supports are necessary for success (seeing a nutritionist, signing up at a gym, taking a meditation class), and then back off, periodically checking in to monitor change, fine-tune the approach, and use accountability as a motivator. The Boot Camp therapist does the same. Is it brief? Absolutely. The assessment and treatment plans are developed in a matter of a few sessions and the client knows exactly what to do. Follow-ups serve only to make sure that clients gain sufficient traction to move ahead on their own.

Counterindications for the Boot Camp Approach

Obviously not everyone will quickly, if ever, gain this traction. Given the model described we need to talk about who is not a good candidate for the Boot Camp approach. Again, the criteria follow those of the brief therapy approach overall:

Clients with severe mental illnesses. Someone who has schizophrenia, untreated bipolar illness or severe major depression, long-standing and untreated OCD, or severe posttraumatic stress obviously needs more than brief treatment. Such persons need to get a handle on their illness, but the illness itself keeps them from carrying through with the criteria mentioned above—the ability to take decisive action, to hit the ground running. They need time for a therapist to help them coordinate additional services—medication; support groups; and help with family, employment, or financial difficulties. Other clients who aren't good candidates for the Boot Camp approach include individuals with untreated eating disorders or addictions.

That said, there are circumstances in which a brief therapy approach for some of these conditions may be all that is needed. Suppose, for example, Mary has a long history of bulimia but has been stable for many years; under the stress of dealing with a sudden relationship breakup, however, she finds herself falling back into her old disordered eating patterns. She knows what to do; she is not in denial; she only needs to some support and accountability to help break this dysfunctional pattern, help her talk through the grief of the breakup, and then move on. This the Boot Camp approach can offer her.

Or Jim, who has had bouts of major depression and begins to feel himself moving in a downward depressive cycle, might come in for support and help with reversing this decline. Like Mary, he may know what to do—talk to his psychiatrist about his medication, talk about stressors that may be aggravating his condition, ramp up what he knows to be positive self-care. After a few sessions he is doing better, and further sessions, spaced out, are used as check-ins to ensure he continues to do what he knows he needs to do and help him stay on track. In a couple of months he feels strong enough to discontinue therapy for now.

Clients who need ongoing support. But Jim could also turn out to be someone who needs ongoing support. Perhaps he is isolated, has no family or has few solid friends, or struggles with daily life because of chronic health problems or intellectual deficiencies. He may not need intensive work on any one particular problem— his problems overall are not severe—but he needs the trust and safety that he has with you in the therapeutic relationship to help him stay stable and think through issues when he begins to feel stuck. These types of clients are also not suitable candidates.

Clients with long-standing patterns of self-injurious behaviors. In a variation on the same theme, clients who cut themselves, or who all too easily fall into anorexia, or who decide to go off their medications, or who fall back into old addictions are not meant to receive brief therapy. Their behaviors may be influenced by environmental issues, such as isolation, a lack of support, family problems, or work stress. So while any one session may go well—yes, I had a good week—it is the relationship and knowing that you are there for them to check in with that helps them stay out of psychological trouble.

Clients seeking more insightful, reflective, long-term approaches. If Linda calls you and says she has thought about beginning therapy for some time and really feels she wants to spend some time unraveling her past, uncovering past traumas, understanding how and why she is who she is, she is not a good candidate for the Boot Camp approach. Rather than wanting to hit the ground running, focus on her present circumstances, and make concrete behavioral changes, she wants to reflect and understand. Obviously she is looking for a different therapy experience and brief therapy is not for her.

Clients who are ambivalent or resistant to therapy. Sam comes to see you because his wife wants him to deal with his anger or his drinking but he quite honestly thinks these are her problems, not his, and he dislikes the idea of talking to strangers about his business. You may want to take the time to orient him to therapy as a whole, to your model, to you. You may want to see if there is a change he really does want to make for himself, or you may even want to encourage him to invite his wife in so her concerns can be discussed in a safe environment.

But after all is said and done, he may still not be a customer. He understands what you're offering but isn't interested, and he's not going to be able to make effective use of the brief therapy process. He may come a few times to appease his wife, and he may or may not make half-hearted attempts to do the homework you suggest, but at the end of the day the changes will be minimal or there will be none at all. The danger here is that you wind up working harder than he does and ultimately will feel frustrated and defeated. Sure, take a bit of time to see if he can engage in some way, but if not, it's best for you both to move on.

The themes here are simple—those who need more support to be successful, who have different expectations and goals from those of the Boot Camp approach, and who are too ambivalent or resistant to the entire process to gain traction should be encouraged to find other approaches to address their problems.

Overview of the Book

The goal of this book is to provide a user-friendly, practical, road-tested guide to the treatment of anger, anxiety, and depression. This is no academic or scholarly text. You will not find an exhaustive review of the literature or any deep discussions on complex theories of psychotherapy. The tools and treatment plans are concrete, the language informal, the approach pragmatic. You are not asked to completely give up your therapeutic style but rather to find ways of adopting and using the concepts of an action-oriented approach in your own ways of working.

Hopefully, you will learn how to think like a brief therapist in terms of focus, assessment, use of sessions, and construction of behavioral goals. Through case examples and vignettes you will understand how to shape those crucial opening sessions and how to track the process tightly to ensure that you and the client are working toward the same end. By quickly identifying the core dynamic and working through the "learning problems" you will help the client see that change is possible. The momentum of therapy unravels clients' dysfunctional patterns and core dynamics that keep them stuck.

Why the focus on anxiety, anger, and depression? One reason is that they are among the most common problems that bring clients into therapy. Another is that they underlie many couple and family issues: couple and family violence; the relentless undertow of stress; the inability to act or the tendency to act out; insufferable loneliness, disconnection, and the existential dread that no one, not even those close to you, understands what makes you tick, what you need, what you are always afraid of.

But the biggest reason of all, perhaps, is that anxiety, anger, and depression so easily morph one into the other—the anxiety beneath the anger, the anger beneath the depression, the depression mingled within the fabric of anxiety. While the goal of all therapy is to ultimately fix whatever it is that the client presents with, we all know that the therapy process is not only to provide solutions but often also to provide new problems. By untangling the emotional mix so that clients have not only a way of making sense of what is troubling them but also a way of attacking the old problem in a new way, therapists can help clients see the problem through a different lens, think about it creatively, and take action that they would not have taken before.

In Chapter 2 we will discuss the core concepts that make up the Boot Camp approach. These will provide our foundation for thinking "brief," for assessment, and for goal setting. In Chapters 3–5 we will discuss, in detail, treatment plans for addressing anxiety, anger, and depression: assessment questions, treatment goals, process issues, and step-by-step road maps for leading clients through the opening sessions. In Chapter 6 we will look at ways of integrating the Boot Camp approach into your own therapeutic style. Again, case examples will illustrate the thinking, along with strategies, techniques, and tools, to help you incorporate the key elements into your own practice.

Let's get started.

CHAPTER TWO

The Big Six: Core Concepts

IN THIS CHAPTER we are going to look at some of the core concepts that form the foundation of the Boot Camp approach. What you will find are a variety of overlapping models and ideas, particularly in the first three concepts, that apply to assessment, treatment, and the managing of the session process. We'll fine-tune the application of these ideas when we talk about the specific treatment maps in Chapters 3–5.

1. Process: How You Do Anything Is How You Do Everything

Back in the 1930s a Japanese psychiatrist named Shoma Morita developed his own form of therapy, which is still being used in Japan today (Reynolds, 1984). Morita was a contemporary of Sigmund Freud, but unlike Freud, who built his theories on Judeo-Christian concepts, Morita used Buddhism as his foundation. Morita felt that Freud, and Western psychology in general, was focusing too much on emotions, in both theory and treatment—constantly tracking the source of our emotions, analyzing their meaning, and deconstructing them in hopes of changing them.

Enough already, said Morita. With his Buddhist approach of acceptance, and sounding almost like a forerunner of cognitive-behavioral therapists, Morita believed that since we can never directly control our emotions and can only somewhat control our thoughts, we need not dwell on these. Instead we need to focus on our behaviors, which are always under our control. The antidote to life's woes and emotional upsets, he believed, was action. "What is the next thing I need to do?" he urged his patients to ask themselves when they were distressed—and then do it.

If you walk out to the parking lot and find that your car has a flat tire, don't get caught up in your annoyance; don't start telling yourself a story about how life is unfair. Change the tire. Once you do, the problem will be solved, and you can feel good about your accomplishment. Proactivity is the key. If we are able to do what we need to do in spite of how we feel, said Morita, if we focus on our sense of purpose, we create a constructive life, and this, in turn, allows us to feel better about ourselves.

Our first concept, "How you do anything is how you do everything," is a well-known phrase that is rooted in Buddhism and echoes Morita's approach. As with Morita, the focus here on behavior and action—the *do*—but it takes it one step further, speaking to both personality and process: the *how* that *you* do. It tells us that the ways in which we approach the world, our problems, and our emotions are broad brushed, that the *anything* becomes *everything* and incorporates a broader concept of process—the *how*. Whether we tend to withdraw, accommodate, get angry, get anxious, or be assertive and proactive, our response is likely to be our modus operandi (MO) for life's ups and downs. If our style works well, we are able to pull ourselves out of the tar pit of emotions and solve our problems. But if it doesn't—if we are too inflexible or if our approach negatively affects those around us, creating ever more problems—we and our lives become stuck.

This is the foundational concept of the Boot Camp approach because we begin our assessment by asking ourselves, "What keeps this person from solving her problems on her own? What is it that keeps him stuck?" Sometimes it is the overwhelming crush of life—severe losses, serious posttraumatic stress. Sometimes it is lack of skill—in parenting, in managing money, in applying and interviewing for jobs. With support and appropriate treatment the losses can heal, the posttraumatic stress gradually resolve. With concrete skill training—in managing a 2-year-old, in setting up a budget, in how to pull together a résumé or present him- or herself for an interview—the client learns to be successful and competent.

But the stuckness is often the *how*, the client's MO. Our goal is to quickly identify this and then help clients change their *how* by action—Morita's focus on behavior. What is further implied by "How you do anything is how you do everything" is that if we help clients change their overall approach, not only will they be able to resolve their presenting problem, but these changes will ripple across other areas of their lives.

This focus on process is often the opposite of what clients present to us. Rather than bringing in the *how* of process and a focus on action, they come in flooded with *what*—heaps of content, the story of their travails, and a centering on emotions—the anger, the depression, the anxiety. The complaints and emotions fuel and carry the narrative along. If you are seeing members of a couple or of a family, their competing narratives quickly turn into courtroom drama—arguments over who said what and when, who has a right to be angry, detailed backstories and the stacking of evidence. Each is looking to you to sort and sift and play judge, deciding whose version is correct, who is to blame, who is the one with the psychological problem.

Or they want your help to feel better—calm my anger, quell my anxiety, reduce my depression. Let me tell you what my husband did to me and how it was unfair, why I didn't deserve to be fired, and if we can talk about it enough, or if you can give me a prescription that will help me feel better, then maybe I can talk to my husband or get off the couch and look for a job.

The client and the Boot Camp therapist are essentially speaking two different languages, embracing two different perspectives. The client says, I need to feel better in order to be able to do something different. The Boot Camp approach (and Morita would agree) says, Do something different and you will feel better. If you keep sitting on the couch rather than look for a job, if you keep ruminating about your husband rather than talk to him, you will continue to feel the same way. The way out—of negative emotions, of problems that are bogging you down—is always action. And, says our first concept, if that action is different from your MO (and it usually is), you will be able to solve other problems on your own as well. The tools and the increased flexibility that clients gain in their approach to problems will help them to better navigate life's future twists and turns.

UNRAVELING THE CORE DYNAMIC

This takes us to the core dynamic mentioned in Chapter 1 that is at the heart of the Boot Camp approach. It is essentially the origin story of the client's MO, connecting childhood wounds and coping styles with present-day struggles with problems. Defining the core dynamic is the focus of assessment and foundation for treatment. Let's walk through it step by step:

- *Everyone walks out of his or her childhood with emotional wounds.* When you think back over your own childhood, what do you feel you learned to be emotionally sensitive to—your mother's criticism or control, your father's inability to listen or his neglect, what? Almost everyone, often through no deliberate fault of his or her parents, becomes wired for some sensitivities that were seen as hurtful. Or stated another way, almost all of us walk out of our childhoods with certain unmet needs—for attention, for being listened to, for appreciation, for greater freedom.
- *These wounds, filtered through the child's mind, create a worldview of the self and others.* The constantly criticized child

decides he is incompetent, a loser, and that people are critical, or that women can be controlling. The neglected child sees herself as insignificant and that men can be neglectful or self-centered.

- *The child develops coping strategies to deal with potential rewounding.* In order to try to prevent being criticized I become good and accommodating; in the face of control I become angry and defensive; feeling neglected, I withdraw or become passive. A child's options are few—get good, get angry, withdraw—because of her own limited power and cognitive-emotional development.

- *The childhood wounds are inevitably triggered in the adult.* Because they remain unhealed, these wounds persist into adulthood. Your sensitivity to them and your worldview ensure that you will find what you are looking for. Your boss fails to respond when you say good morning when passing her in the hallway, and rather than thinking that she just didn't hear you or is preoccupied, you automatically think that she is upset with you because, you learned, that's how people in authority treat you.

- *The triggering of the wound causes the adult to revert back to his or her childhood coping style.* Your boss's nonresponse causes you to once again feel like a 10-year-old, and your old 10-year-old's response kicks in. Assuming she is annoyed, you offer to take on the extra assignment, or you withdraw and become anxious, or you get angry, taking your anger out on colleagues or customers. If you become upset enough, perhaps, you think about quitting your job.

- *You develop a high tolerance for the wounding behaviors of others.* Even if your boss is truly a critical person, you are apt to endure her criticism longer than others might because it fits your worldview. Your ineffective coping style keep you trapped in this negative loop—feeling rewounded, hating it, yet unable to effectively change it.

The past is constantly re-created in the present, and our sensitivity and response—how you do anything is how you do everything—presents seemingly new problems based on the same process and outcome. We become stuck because what saved us in childhood is not flexible enough for the larger, more complex adult world. Each time the 10-year-old's strategy is triggered, it succeeds in only continuing to perpetuate the 10-year-old's feelings and outlook and prevents real problem solving in the present. We are like computers running on outdated, ineffective software. We need to upgrade our psychological software—our responses, our coping strategies—if we are to break out of the cycle of rewounding.

The notion of childhood wounds has been addressed by others. Harville Hendrix (2007), for example, makes the reigniting of childhood wounds the core of his Imago approach, and he spends a considerable amount of time tracking its impact on couple relationships. However, while Hendrix identifies childhood wounds and seeks to drain these old emotions of their power by going back into each partner's past, the Boot Camp approach handles these issues through behavioral change in the present. Rather than falling back into old ways of coping, Boot Camp clients can begin to rewire their brains and upgrade the software by concretely doing something different.

We can uncover this core dynamic quickly as part of our assessment by noticing and asking about sensitivities when clients present their opening stories. Why did they feel so upset about their boss's reaction? What are they particularly sensitive to in others? What is it, they feel, that others don't or can't give them? What do they do when these feelings arise? What do they feel they needed most from their parents but did not receive?

The upgrading is usually very simple, if emotionally difficult at first. If the goal is to become more flexible, clients need to recognize their sensitivities and responses, understand that these are rooted in the past, and realize that their worldview, however understandable, is limited and distorted. Then they need to do something different, usually just the opposite of what they normally do. If they tend to accommodate, for example, they need to take time to figure out what they want, rather than trying to figure out what they think others want, take the risk of stating what they want, and then take concrete action toward getting it. If they tend to get angry, they need to learn to self-regulate, calming themselves down. Then, rather than merely biting their tongues, they need to use their anger as information about what they need, take the risk of assertively expressing their needs (what they could not do as a child), and again take concrete action toward meeting them. If they tend to withdraw, they need to move forward, in spite of how they feel, and again speak up and assert their needs.

By doing this not only are the number of tools in their emotional toolbox expanded, but also they begin to feel less like 10-year-olds, and more empowered, countering feelings of anxiety, anger, and depression. By being assertive and stating what they need—appreciation, reassurance, attention, opportunities for independent action and decisions—they are doing now with others what they could not do with their parents. Each time they are able to do this, their views of themselves and the world are changed, and their childhood wounds begin to heal. With time and practice, they become less sensitive and feel less trapped, and, as Morita would say, they create a productive life that they can feel good about.

The implications of this first concept and its tie to the client's core dynamic means, then, that process, for both you, the therapist, and the client, is more important than content. In fact, content becomes relatively unimportant. You and the client don't need to spend time piecing together all the elements of the story, digging through the details of past events and facts, or wasting time in couple or family sessions figuring out whether it was really Tuesday or Wednesday. Instead of the *what*, you and the client only need focus on the *how*—helping clients in the here-and-now to take steps to change their MO.

You focus your skills on making sure that you and clients are on this same page—tracking the process like a bloodhound—so that they understand this shift from content to process and see how changing the process will change their presenting problems. Here you say that if you keep doing the same thing, you will keep feeling the same way. Once they are on board with you, you then focus on a treatment plan that encourages them to take concrete action outside their comfort zone, that behaviorally changes their response and breaks the childhood patterns. According to this first principle, once they change anything, they change everything.

So no, clients don't need to have the dreaded conversation with their mother or spouse after the first session if that seems too overwhelming. They can start slow. If the goal, for example, is to speak up rather than withdraw, they can start with the salesperson at 7-Eleven who gives them the wrong change, or their office mate who talks too loud and interrupts their work. The goal isn't about getting the right change or having a quieter office but speaking up, even though a client's instincts tell him or her to let it go. When clients find out that what they feared doesn't happen—that the sales clerk doesn't become enraged, that the office colleague doesn't refuse to ever talk to them again—brain rewiring begins and larger steps can be taken. Once clients begin to change their core dynamic—healing wounds by changing their response—their approach to life and its problems is forever altered.

2. Be Adult

If changing the *how*—the core dynamic—gives us the direction, the concept of being adult gives us the destination. It tells us where we want to be, and it also provides us with a model of good mental health.

As mentioned in Chapter 1, the brief therapist is similar to the physician. If you go to the doctor with a fever, for example, she may do lab tests. She'll know if your blood count is off, for example, because she has a standard range against which to measure it. If it is too high or too low, she can use this information to not only form her diagnosis and treatment but also educate you, the patient, about the problem and possible solution.

In the same way the physician relies on lab standards to indicate illness, the Boot Camp therapist measures a client's mental health against the standard of the adult. It offers not only a tool for assessment but also a goal that the therapist can help the client move toward. It is similar to Bowen's differentiated self, the ability to have a clear sense of one's values, beliefs, and principles and to be able to hold on to them in the face of anxiety, togetherness, and the pressure to conform (Bowen, 1978; Gilbert & Gilbert, 1992). It is authenticity, integrity.

This concept provides a solid footing for action-oriented treatment. The best way to talk about this is to describe what is called the *relationship triangle* and show how the adult navigates these dynamics differently. This model overlaps with our discussion of process and core dynamic. Think of it as a further expansion of those concepts.

THE RELATIONSHIP TRIANGLE

The relationship triangle is a variation and expansion on the original *drama triangle*, also known as the *Karpman triangle*, which was developed by psychiatrist Steven Karpman (1968) (Fig. 2.1). Let's walk through the overall dynamic, then discuss its implications for the Boot Camp approach.

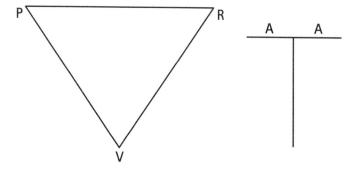

Figure 2.1

The triangle commonly describes the relationship between two people and the way they can alternate between three different roles. The *P* (persecutor), *R* (rescuer), and *V* (victim) represent the different roles that the people can play; it is not the people themselves but a role. The roles are interdependent and there is always someone on top, who seems to have more power, and someone on the bottom. The relationship moves about in a circle as follows:

The person in the R position is the rescuer. The person in that role essentially has "nice guy" control. He hooks into the V, or victim. The victim feels overwhelmed at times, that problems are falling down on his head. The rescuer steps in and says, "I can help you out. Just do what I say, everything will be fine." Oftentimes couples will begin their relationship in some form of this. They psychologically cut a deal: The rescuer says, I will agree to be big, strong, good, and nice; the victim says, I will agree to be overwhelmed and unable to manage. The victim has someone to lean on; the rescuer feels needed and in charge. Everyone is happy.

And it works fine, except every once in a while one of two things happens. Sometimes the rescuer gets tired of doing it all. She feels as though she is shouldering all the responsibilities and that the other is not pulling her weight, not giving anything back, not appreciating what the rescuer is doing. The rescuer periodically gets fed up, angry, resentful. Bam! She shifts over to the P, persecutor, role. She suddenly blows up, usually about something minor such as laundry or trash, or acts out, goes out and spends a lot of money, goes on a drinking binge, has an affair. She feels she deserves it. She says to herself, "Look at what I've been putting up with." The message underneath the behavior and anger that usually does not come out clearly is "Why don't you grow up! Why don't you take some responsibility! Why do I have to do everything around here! Why don't you appreciate what I am doing for you? This is unfair!" The feeling of unfairness is a strong one.

When this explosion or acting out happens, the victim understandably gets scared, moves up to the R position, and tries to make up to calm the waters. "I'm sorry," he says. "I didn't realize. I really do appreciate what you do. I'll do better." Then the persecutor/rescuer feels bad about whatever he did or said and goes down to the victim position and gets depressed. Then R and V both stabilize and go back to their original positions.

But sometimes the victim gets tired of being on the bottom. She gets tired of the other one always running the show, always telling her what to do. She gets tired of being looked down on because the rescuer is basically saying, "If it wasn't for me, you wouldn't make it." Every once in a while the victim gets fed up and, bam, moves to the persecutor role. Like the rescuer, the victim in this role blows up and gets angry, usually about something small, or acts out on themselves, self-destructively, or on others.

The message underneath that doesn't get said clearly is "Why don't you get off my back! Leave me alone, stop controlling my life! Back off, I can do things myself!" Should the rescuer hear this, he then moves to the victim position. He says to himself, "Poor me, every time I try to help, look what I get." The victim/persecutor then feels bad about whatever he did or said and goes to the rescuer position and says something like, "I was stressed out, off my meds, tired from the kids. I'm sorry." And then they make up and go back to where they originally were.

While everyone gets to move between all the roles, often a person will fit more comfortably into one role more than another. This has to do with personality, upbringing, and learned childhood ways of coping. The rescuer as a child was often an only child, was the oldest, or grew up in a chaotic family. She usually did not have many buffers between herself and her parents and learned early on that she could avoid getting in trouble and avoid conflict by being good: If I can stay on my toes and just do what my parents (and teacher) wants me to do all the time, I won't get in any hot water.

This type of person learned to be very sensitive to others as a means of survival. He developed good radar and could pick up the nuances of emotions. He became hyperalert, spending all his energy surveying the environment, staying on his toes, ever ready to do what his parents wanted. Essentially he took the stance of "I'm happy if you're happy, and I need to make sure you're happy." And it pays off—he gets praised for being a good kid.

What works for the child, however, doesn't necessarily work so well for the adult. Now the world is bigger, the software outdated. Rather than just two or three important people to pay attention to and please, the adult rescuer has many more—her boss, her partner, the lady from church, the president of the local Rotary Club. She now feels pulled in a lot of directions, stretched thin, as she scrambles to accommodate what she thinks others want from her. She easily feels like a martyr, is always at risk of burnout.

She also has a hard time knowing what she wants. She knows what she should do; she has a laundry list in her head running 24/7 telling her what she ought to do. But because she spent so much of her energy as a child looking outward and doing what others wanted, she never had the opportunity to sit back and decide what she wanted. Wanting, unlike following shoulds and rules, is a feeling, and she is often not aware of what she is feeling. As an adult if you ask her, "But what do you want?" she hesitates and gets stuck. She worries about making the right decision, about not offending anyone in her life, or most of all about arousing the critical voice in her head.

She also has a hard time with anger and conflict (which is why she became good in the first place) and tends to stuff anger down until she gets fed up and begins to gag on it. Then she blows up and goes to P, but because she is so uncomfortable with the turmoil and drama it creates, she eventually feels guilty. She shoves it all back down again, only to have it build up again.

The victim, in contrast, was as a child often the youngest in the family, was overprotected or micromanaged by parents, or had older siblings who stepped in and took over all the time when he was stuck with a problem. What he missed in growing up were opportunities to develop the self-confidence that comes from learning to manage problems on your own. Now, as an adult, he easily gets overwhelmed, feels unconfident, anxious. To handle these feelings he looks to the rescuer, who takes over and helps him feel better.

Finally, there are those whose primary stance is that of a persecutor. Think of her as the evil twin of the rescuer. Whereas the rescuer controls by being good and nice, the persecutor is angry, critical, and blaming. This person is the abuser, controlling everyone and everything around her in an angry aggressive manner as a way of ensuring that no one sneaks up and gets her from behind. Some couples start out with an abusive persecutor-victim relationship, playing out childhood models and roles.

Let's look at the diagram of the *As* (see Fig. 2.1). These folks stand outside the triangle. The *A* stands for "adult" and is similar to Bowen's differentiated self. The adults are not in a role. In contrast to those in the triangle, these individuals, as represented by the diagram, are at the same level of power; they are peers. The vertical line between them signifies clear personal boundaries. They are proactive rather than reactive, self-responsible rather than blaming, able to be emotionally calm even when the other person is upset. They are able to step back and see problems in the relationship and make positive changes without any expectations of the other; they see others as anxious or fearful rather than malicious or manipulative in conflict; they are able to not react in kind to anger or another's anxiety; they are able to hold to their values and choices even if others disagree or are disapproving (Gilbert & Gilbert, 1992).

Essentially the mindset of the adult is "I'm responsible for what I think, do, say. If something bothers me, it is *my* problem. If you can do something to help me with *my* problem, I need to tell you, because you can't read my mind. If you decide, for whatever reason, not to help me, I'll need to decide what I'm going to do next to fix my problem. Similarly, if something bothers you, it is *your* problem. If there is something I can do to help you with your problem, you need to tell me. And if I decide not to help you with *your* problem, you're an adult, you can work it out. You may not handle it the way I might, but you can do it. I don't need to take over."

Two of the problems the rescuer and victim have in their relationship is that they do expect a lot of mind reading—you should know what is going on or how to help without my having to explain—and then feel frustrated or disappointed or angry when the other does not. They also have a distorted sense of responsibility: The rescuer tends to be overresponsible—your problems are my problems; I'm happy if you are happy and I actually feel anxious when you are not. Partly because I care and partly to relieve my anxiety, my first response when you are upset is to do something to make you feel better. In the attempt to "make" the victim happy, the victim over time begins to feel pressure and control, which sets up the explosion. The overresponsibility of the rescuer is countered by the underresponsibility of the victim: My problems are your problems. I expect you to fix them, and I either have to wait or manipulate you into doing so.

The adults, in contrast, are clear about who has the problem. If you feel it, it's yours. By being aware of who has the problem, the individuals can avoid the defensiveness, anxiety, control, and manipulation of those caught in the triangle.

The adults are also able to be more intimate. The problem the rescuer and victim face in their relationship is that the roles keep them stuck. The rescuer cannot let down his guard or get too vulnerable because he is afraid that the victim will not be able to handle it. Similarly, the victim cannot ever get too strong because the rescuer will feel threatened and out of job. The long line in the triangle running from the victim and rescuer is real, representing the emotional distance between them. The adults, in contrast, don't have this problem. Both can be responsible, strong, and yet honest and vulnerable. They can take risks, are not locked in roles, and hence, can be more open.

Now, obviously the relationship triangle has wide implications for couple relationships. It helps to explain the periodic explosions that couples can get into, as well as affairs and other acting out. It also explains how couples need to change over time to be successful—namely, to both move toward the adult stance. But it also ties into the core dynamic and common sources of anxiety, anger, and depression. We can glean from the model several other perspectives that can help us with our assessment and treatment.

THE WORLD OF Rs

Many of our clients easily cast themselves into the role of rescuers, the Rs. Such individuals often give the appearance of being in control and, at times, controlling of others, but underneath are struggling. Their learned sensitivity to the emotions of others, their instinct to always do the right thing, to please others, to make others happy, not only leaves them feeling like martyrs but also always walking on eggshells. Their difficulty with confrontation and conflict causes them to internalize many of their feelings; they struggle with decisions, leaving them anxious and on guard.

Essentially Rs operate on childlike magical thinking: If I do everything that I am supposed to do, then people will somehow know what I need and give it to me without my asking. Obviously in the complex adult world, others don't know what they need, hence the martyr behavior and eventual resentment. Under stress their first line of defense is to be "good" and accommodating. Under even more stress they get "gooder," trying even harder until they collapse or become resentful and explode. They also invariably set themselves up for further resentment by thinking, "If I am always doing what I think I should do, I expect that others should also be doing what I think they should do." When others don't do what Rs think they should, they get resentful, feel the unfairness.

The other variation is, If I am always doing what I think I should do, I expect some payoff, some reward (for example, if I work extra I will get a promotion at work; if I mow the lawn I'll have sex with my partner). Again invariably the rescuer gets resentful because others don't automatically know that the R is doing what she is doing because she should. They often assume that she is doing what she is doing because she wants to (takes on the extra assignment because she enjoys the challenge, mows the lawn because she likes how it looks).

But again, under it all is anxiety and oversensitivity to others. Rather than sorting out the wants from the shoulds, the R is locked in his own mindset. This explains the generalized anxiety that many clients present with, as well as their intermittent anger or acting out. It even explains their control of others. It is their anxiety and their difficulty with transitions that lead to their control and their irritability when others suggest or do things that they hadn't already planned out in their minds.

THE WORLD OF Vs

The Vs' perspective from the bottom of the triangle leaves them projecting their power on others, seeing them as bigger and stronger than them. They too are anxious, not because they are always trying to please others, but because they lack self-confidence and skills in dealing with the world. They are reactive and when flooded with anxiety lean on others. But with the leaning also comes the loss of control over their own lives. They may present to therapy as feeling overwhelmed by others, by life's problems, and they also present with depression because they often feel trapped and helpless. While their dependency on others can be comforting at first (in the early years of close relationships, at the start of therapy), the controlling aspect of the others takes its toll. As with Rs, their difficulty articulating their needs and sense of powerlessness leads to their "taking what they get until they can't take it anymore," leading to their periodic resentment, explosions, or acting out—toward others, or toward themselves in the form of self-destructive behaviors.

THE WORLD OF Ps

The persecutors who occupy this role most of the time are those who are aggressive and controlling, but like the Rs are often driven by hypervigilance and anxiety. They present to therapy with anger management issues and are seen as callous and abusive by others. Like the Rs and Vs, they project onto others what they are not aware of in themselves. They are not as angry and tough as they think but see their underside in the Vs and Rs. Like them they need to incorporate these traits—greater sensitivity, greater vulnerability.

Working within these roles helps us see the intimate connections between anxiety, anger, and depression. By asking pointed questions about their feelings of being trapped or overwhelmed (Vs); accommodating, anxious, and driven (Rs); limited in their emotional range and aggressive (Ps), we can assess and explain to clients where problems arise in relationships and how anger, anxiety, and depression interplay. It also clearly ties to our first concept—How you do anything is how you do everything—and the individual's core dynamic.

THE WORLD OF ADULTS

The adults are where we want our clients to be; this is our measure of good mental health and our road map for treatment. Adults are able to bypass the potholes that the Rs, Vs, and Ps can fall into. Because adults see others as peers, because they are sensitive yet have firm boundaries, they are able to be assertive with others about their needs. Because they are proactive rather than reactive, are able to be responsible for and solve their own problems, they are less prone to the anxiety of doing good and being hypervigilant, the powerlessness and trapped feeling of depression, or the aggression of anger and resentment.

Just as the physician uses the lab results to know where patients need to be, we can use the adult model to guide clients and treatment to where they need to be. The simple question that clinicians need to always ask themselves is the variation of the bumper sticker question "What would Jesus or Buddha do?" Instead the Boot Camp therapist asks, "What would an adult do?" We quickly can discern what that is—move out of the roles, often do the opposite of what is normally done, act in ways that are less explosive, controlling, and accommodating, that are more em-powering, assertive, and responsible.

3. Look for the Holes

Our third concept carries forward the foundation we laid down in the first two. If the first helps us focus on process and the undoing of childhood coping and wounds, and the second gives us a model and map for where we want to go, "Look for the holes" tells us how to both focus the process and move individuals toward the adult stance.

USING THE PROCESS

There is a concept in art known as "negative space." If you are painting a picture of an orange, the orange is the positive space and the area around the orange is the negative space. In therapy, the Boot Camp therapist is always looking for the negative space—the holes—what is in the background, what is not talked about rather than what is. For a family that is always talking about their troublesome son Tom who acts out at school, but never talks about when he does well, the hole is those positive aspects and memories. For the members of a couple who always talk about anger but never about the soft emotions like hurt or worry or affection, the hole is the soft emotions. Individuals who always talk about their past or their father but never about the future or their mother, the hole is the future or the mother. Essentially we want to go where the client is not. We want to be curious and ask questions about what clients are not talking about.

Why? Because usually what clients talk about is familiar ground, well within their comfort zone. The family knows the negative story of Tom; the couple probably has been having the same type of argument for 10 years; the individual is holding on to the past or his or her father. The Boot Camp approach is about breaking up and breaking out of patterns, moving toward the uncomfort-able and unknown. The process goal is to stir the pot, to ask the hard questions that clients are afraid to ask or can't articulate. By noticing what is not being said, we begin to change the narrative, help clients see different aspects of the problems, which can, in turn, mobilize their energy and focus.

In addition to topics, we are looking for what clients can't quite say. This is the subtle awareness of language—the way John mentions "problems" or "things in the past." How Ellen stops and shifts gears in midsentence—"And then he . . . but the teacher said"—or simply trails off. To be aware of this is to see language working as protection. To talk about "a problem" rather than specifically describing the behavior or situation is to put a protective glaze over the emotions. To stop in midsentence and shift course is to "not go there." So go there; ask, "What problems?" "What things?" Ask the client to go back and finish the sentence. The more specific the language becomes, the more defined become the emotions.

This is what allows you to drop a line into the clients' deeper emotional waters and discover what is there. And as we will discuss later in our treatment plans, this is the antidote to anger, anxiety, and depression—to create in the session process a greater emotional range and with it new cognitions.

Finally, this is what you can always do when you get stuck—move toward the blind spots, into that uncharted territory where both their anxiety and healing lie. Ask yourself what you would expect to see or hear that you're not. With practice what's presented will become an automatic springboard for zeroing in on what's not.

MOVING TOWARD THE ADULT

Looking for the holes also complements our relationship triangle model and core dynamics: What keeps the client from being an adult, what does the client needs to do that she is not doing, what is he not showing right here in the room?

Again, what you will hear in the opening narrative of rescuers is the burden of overresponsibility, the high sensitivity to others, the accommodation, the martyr type of behavior, the language of *shoulds*. You will notice that they are constantly walking on egg-shells with others, even with you—exhibiting a hypersensitivity to you and what you say, the niceness and reasonableness that is part and parcel of their persona.

Focus on what is lacking, what is not presented in the room. Ask about what they want rather than what they should do, about times of decisive action rather than walking on eggshells, about bursts of anger rather than niceness and being good. Ask directly: "I hear what you should do, but what do you want? You're worrying about what others may think, but what do you want to do? What do you do when you get angry?" These questions are often difficult for them to answer. They will get anxious, try to figure out the right answer they need to give you, but you need to ask them anyway to move them out of their comfort zone, toward the adult.

For victims, you will sense their powerlessness, a cascading of problems that fall on them. They will talk about being anxious and depressed and how their emotions run their lives. They feel stuck and can't do what they need to do because of how awful they feel. They will look to you to alleviate these feelings, to bail them out in some way, to take over. What's missing is an ability to partialize problems or override and relieve their powerlessness through action. So you focus on these: Breaking the lump of problems into smaller bits—their boss, their wife, their worry about money. You work together with them to come up with a plan of action that they can do now, today, accomplish this week—send an email to their boss, talk to their wife, balance their checkbook. Help them use action as the antidote to their stuckness.

And for those who present themselves as primarily persecutors, you hear the wall of anger, the blaming of others for their anger and their bullying behavior as a way of coping with problems. What will be missing is their lack of emotional range, one that that includes softer emotions, their lack of self-responsibility, and lack of ability to regulate their anger. This is what you focus on;

ask, "Can you tell when you are sad, worried, or anxious?" Challenge them to use their anger as information about their needs and problems to solve, rather than as a weapon against others. Confront them on the need to self-regulate and work with them to quickly come up with a plan to do exactly that.

Looking for the holes means that in that first session you are both assessing for and zeroing in on what is left out of their repertoire of adult behaviors. One additional challenge is staying in the adult role yourself.

THE THERAPIST AS THE ADULT

Effectively focusing on the holes and moving individuals toward the adult stance means that you need to do the same. You need to be able to sidestep the dangers of being dragged into the relationship triangle yourself. So when dealing with persecutors, for example, you need to not become the victim—feel bullied or intimidated, give up your own power and leadership—but instead push back, challenge their stance without sounding aggressive yourself so as not to seem threatening.

For victims, it means not rescuing them by taking over—offering to call and invite their spouse to the next session, for example, rather than asking them to do it—and certainly not being bullying yourself by being aggressive or demanding. It also means being careful that you are not pulled into their tar pit of emotions, feeling overwhelmed or confused by the heap of problems, feeling the undertow of powerlessness that leaves you wallowing, stuck, and unsure how to proceed. As with persecutors, you need to remain clearheaded and rational. You need to make your case for planning and action and work together with them toward concrete steps of success.

Finally, with rescuers, your challenge is not triggering their "good kid" accommodation and pleasing passivity in response to your perceived power and authority. You want to be clear but careful that you do not overly confront them. If you sense the accommodation—the too ready agreement with what you are saying, a passivity—you know you have a problem in the room. Their core dynamic has been triggered; their anxiety is up. You need to lower it by gently commenting on what has happened and reassuring them that you are interested in helping them accomplish what they want rather than what they think *you* want.

This knowing how you need to be and not be in the opening session and how to successfully steer the session process is the skill, as well as the artistry, of doing all therapy. But in the Boot Camp approach this is essential in order to hit the ground running. The heightened focus on process, the framework of the relationship triangle, and the concepts of holes in the session provide a map of the terrain. We'll drill down to the details of shaping the process in subsequent chapters.

4. Don't Do It Right, Do It Differently (There Are No Mistakes)

If you are worried about making mistakes you become anxious. If you are critical of yourself for making mistakes you tend to be depressed. If you believe others shouldn't make mistakes you become angry.

We've all heard the phrase *ready, aim, fire*, but the reality check is *ready, fire, aim*. This latter phrase is used as a mainstay of improv, where spontaneity is the goal. It is also real life, where we learn and develop solutions from trial and error. Mistakes are what we can determine only after the fact. When Steve Jobs worked in his garage creating a new computer, he did so with no idea of what would happen next. It could have flopped, been too complex or expensive for an everyday world built on paper, adding machines, and phones. We take the best action we can, see what happens next, and adjust, because the outcome is out of our control. This is part of the creative process, the tinkering that comes as we get feedback about what works and what doesn't, whether it be the experience at the party, the conversation with our spouse, the design of a new fashion line. This perspective is found in the well-known inspirational quotation "Good decisions come from experience, and experience comes from making bad decisions."

It is this fear that clients have about the fallout of their mistakes that the Boot Camp approach sets out to undo. We need to help them learn not to worry about doing it right and just to do it differently. The behavioral breaking out of habits and patterns, the stepping out of comfort zones and expanding one's tolerance for risk and the anxiety that comes with it is paramount—again, process, not content. The fine-tuning can come later.

You can easily help clients with this not only by helping them see how their thinking and emotions are interfering with their ability to solve the problems they are facing, but also by educating them about the problem-solving process itself: Decide what it is you want to do or say and then do it. That is Part 1. Then see what happens next—Part 2. The other person gets angry or quiet or the CD that you decided to buy turns out to be lousy. New problem—the other is upset or has misunderstood you; you realize you don't really like that band's music. It doesn't mean that you shouldn't have done Part 1; it just means that you need to address the new problem—explain again your intentions, listen to what the other is saying, decide not to buy any more music from that group or sell it back to the store. Don't beat yourself up, but instead pat yourself on the back for taking the risk.

This obviously applies to therapists as well. Beginning therapists in particular are prone to the same worries and caution—that they can't make an interpretation, suggest a course of action, confront a client until they have assembled enough information to know what it is right. You can't and don't want to do that with brief therapy; it is pragmatic and interactive. Make your interpretation—"It sounds like your boss reminds you of your mother"—and then see what happens next. If the client makes a face or says, "Yes, but," there is a new problem. The interpretation didn't work; there is a problem in the room; fix the problem before going ahead. Say, "It seems as though you don't agree," or "I'm saying this because . . ." and see what happens next and whether the client is back in step with you. You can't make a mistake.

5. Problems Are Bad Solutions

Natasha comes to therapy with her husband, Carl, because Natasha thinks Carl is an alcoholic—he drinks a quart of vodka every night. It's likely that Carl doesn't think his drinking is a problem. For him it is a solution to another, often unspoken problem—that he is depressed, or worried about money, or angry at Natasha for always nagging and criticizing him.

To say that problems are bad solutions means that you are always curious about what is beneath the problem that clients present, that there are dynamics in place that clients are unaware of and that you want to decipher. Addictions are bad solutions, affairs are bad solutions, and so at some level are anger, anxiety, and depression.

Here we move into therapeutic models—psychodynamic theories point you toward the past, for example, while systems point you toward relationship interactions—and in the Boot Camp approach we are looking at missing skills, faulty process, the roles of the triangle, core dynamics, failure to act. But the focus is not about making the "right" causal connection. Like looking for the holes, seeing problems as solutions becomes a fulcrum for change. By our always being curious about what lies beneath a problem, we not only are peeling away new layers of problems that help us with our assessment and treatment planning; we are helping clients to do the same.

Seeing problems as bad solutions also helps clients step out of the who-what-where-good-bad content and judgment in their heads. It enables them to consider a broader view, a new narrative that can mobilize energy. Using the relationship triangle, for example, rescuing-prone clients can understand how their angry explosions are not "out of the blue" or an imitation of their parent but reflect the culmination of resentment and unmet needs. Similarly, anxiety makes sense when underneath it is a fear of confrontation and inability to be assertive. Depression is not just a lead weight that drags one down and has no explanation but is the result of critical voices, feeling trapped in a vise of real circumstances, or the undertow of grief that lingers and remains unresolved.

Therapy ultimately is about helping clients find solutions but usually begins by giving them new problems—a new perspective that both mobilizes them and challenges them to think differently and break out of old patterns. While having treatment strategies is valuable, you, as the therapist, do not have to have all the answers. Your goal is to change the process and focus by asking clients hard questions: "If . . . is a bad solution, what do you think is the problem?" And then see what happens next.

6. Be Honest

If you, as the therapist, don't know what to say in a session, say, "I don't know what to say." If therapy seems stuck, say, "It seems like we're stuck." We associate honesty with the unbarring of one's soul, the hyperintimate conversation in which you reveal deep secrets. Beginning therapists often confuse honesty with excessive self-disclosure. But as with the other concepts, being honest is about keeping your fingers on the pulse of the process. You notice how Sam makes a face after you offer an interpretation and you stop to see what he is feeling and take the time to clarify. You talk about your intentions, help the client understand your thinking: "I'm asking about this because I'm wondering . . . "; "I'm suggesting you do this for homework because I think it will help you . . ." You are the one to talk about the elephant in the room—the holes—that others can't or pretend not to see.

By doing this you are doing a couple of things. First, you are being a model for good communication. As mentioned earlier, many clients associate good communication with good content, the stacking up of "correct" facts and evidence, and often overtalk by saying more of the same thing. Those prone to anxiety associate good communication with the "right" answer, figuring out what to say to not get others upset, and can undertalk, not say enough for fear of saying the wrong thing. Good communication is about talking sincerely and completely: letting others know your intentions, that is, what the emotion, need, or concern is that sparks your comment; taking responsibility for what you say by making *I* statements, that is, using "adult" communication rather than talking about the other (what angry people tend to do); and, finally, being sensitive to their reaction to see if your comment was misunderstood and received differently from what you intended (ready, fire, aim).

Good therapeutic communication also often has an element of risk—the quick flutter of anxiety—that signals that you are moving out of your comfort zone. This is essentially the definition of intimacy, not the revealing of the dark secret of what happened to me when I was 5 years old, but saying what feels difficult to say—I don't want to do this; this is what I need—and saying it anyway. This is what clients need to do—move into the holes—to deepen their conversations. If you can do this, you model how they can do it.

Being honest with this type of communication also helps clients learn how to be sensitive to and use process. Having conversations is like driving a car. There are two parts to driving a car. One is knowing where you are going—what is it that I want the other person to most understand about me, what is it I need, what problem we need to most resolve by the end of this conversation—that is, having clear intentions. The other is keeping the car on the road. This is where clients often have the most trouble. Within 3 minutes the couple are talking about Christmas 2006, or somebody's mother, or who did what when. Your job as therapist is to help clients keep the car on the road—stay on topic, stay focused, be clear.

Often you can do this by simply stopping the process and saying, "I'm getting confused; I don't understand what the connection is between . . ." or "You started talking about . . . but now you're talking about . . . I'm having a hard time connecting the dots." By tracking the process and letting clients know when the conversation is going off the road, you help them begin to do that themselves. This makes for more productive conversations because the client is not drifting off into the weeds of old, well-known topics, and when combined with your tapping unspoken emotions, the conversations become deeper and more intimate and have greater emotional impact.

Finally, like the other concepts, being honest is what you do when you're not sure what to do. Talk about your thinking, about the process that just unfolded, about the holes, rather than mentally scrabbling to have the right answer, the perfect insight.

This wraps up our discussion of the six key concepts. Again, it's easy to see how they overlap and offer a way of navigating the assessment and treatment process. In Chapter 3 we'll discuss how to apply these as we describe the treatment map for anxiety. We'll describe the general format for Boot Camp opening sessions, examining the overall Boot Camp approach to anxiety, and finally describe the actual process and content of those sessions with anxious clients.

Treatment Map for Anxiety

IT STARTS OUT INNOCENTLY ENOUGH. Ellen goes online to find a flea treatment for her dog. But 5 hours later she is still at it with no end in sight. She's worried that she hasn't found the "best" one, that there is always lurking on the next site another product that is better, that she will wind up regretting whatever decision she makes. While at some level she realizes that what she is doing is overkill, she feels she can't stop it.

Tom, a college student, is planning on attending the year-end gala fraternity dinner and dance and is scared to death. He's always felt awkward around anyone other than family and his closest friend. He fears "making a fool of himself" or getting so upset that he might get sick to his stomach and not be able to last the night.

Terese says that she has always had a "problem with her nerves." Her mind is constantly running; she worries a lot, about her health, about money; and she easily feels overwhelmed by daily life events— her daughter being angry with her, the dog barking, an unexpected bill. On bad days she takes Klonopin for her anxiety or goes to sleep to get away from it all.

Such examples show three of the common faces of anxiety. In this chapter we are going to explore the treatment of these and other forms of anxiety. While in Chapter 2 we discussed the broad structure of the Boot Camp model and key concepts that serve as its foundation, in this chapter we will be drilling down to the microlevel, seeing how foundational ideas translate into the active treatment of anxiety.

Moving toward that microlevel, this chapter also serves as a template of sorts for the basic goals, tools, and techniques that apply across the board to anxiety, anger, and depression. We will, for example, talk in more detail here about the goals and process of that important first session, ways of changing the emotional climate, various types of self-regulation techniques, and the use of homework. Having laid down this base, we will highlight the variations that will apply when we move to anger and depression.

Finally, this chapter is structurally divided into three parts. In the first part we'll look at the Boot Camp approach to anxiety—the focus, goals, and treatment tasks. In the second part we'll lay out the overall structure of the all-important initial contact and first session as they apply not only to anxiety but also to anger and depression. Finally, we'll walk through the opening sessions specific to treating anxiety. Along the way we'll show how to put into practice the concepts mentioned in the previous chapters—tracking the process like a bloodhound, changing the emotional climate, defining the core dynamic, and using homework to ground skills and begin the brain-rewiring process.

The Boot Camp Approach to Anxiety

There has been much research in past years about brain processes and anxiety, readily available through not only academic journals but also YouTube videos and websites devoted to anxiety relief and treatment. We now know that a highly active amygdala generates feelings of anxiety and also can override the prefrontal cortex and the rational mind. We know there is a genetic component, with anxiety running in families; that trauma and childhood abuse and neglect can hot-wire the amygdala at an early age (Child Welfare Information Gateway, 2009); and that now, thanks to brain plasticity, individuals can learn to rewire their brains and reshape their personalities.

The Boot Camp approach to anxiety aims to rewire both brain and personality in a direct behavioral way through a three-pronged focus, as described below.

Recognizing the Anxious State of Mind

We are now in the "third wave" of behavioral therapy, moving from straight behavioral approaches, with their negative rewards and operant conditioning; to the Cognitive Behavioral Therapy of Aaron Beck, with its focus on the deconstruction of thoughts themselves; to the current focus on states of mind (Siegel, 2011). Using this framework, we don't need to spend time tracking down the details of clients' thoughts—"This is *awful*"; "I *always* screw up!"—but rather help clients recognize when anxiety (or anger or depression) and an overactive amygdala are overrunning the prefrontal lobe, so they can take corrective action.

Identifying this state of mind isn't all that's hard to do. We all have familiarity with the voice of anxiety—the worry about the future, the expectation of disaster, the nagging fear that drags at us like an undertow, the queasy stomach and shakiness. This is what we hear in the first session, the clients' renditions of anxiety in their lives: Ellen describing how she is getting lost in the Internet world, unable to walk away from some inner push to find that perfect product; Tom replaying over and over scenes of distress and humiliation at his fraternity party; Terese feeling "shaky inside," her worries coming down on top of her like an avalanche, only knowing how to stop it by popping a Klonopin or trying to go to sleep.

We don't want or need to get in the thick of details—what exactly Ellen does or thinks when she is stuck on the computer, what specifically Tom imagines, why the barking dog or the unexpected bill throws Terese off course. We only need to identify the broad contours of clients' anxiety and help them do the same—hours on the Internet, scenes of the party, the feeling of being overwhelmed. This, we say, is what anxiety is—the thinking in the future, the what-ifs, the sense that everything is important, that everything is a potential problem, that you need to be on guard. This is your ramped-up amygdala overrunning your rational mind, and for you it centers around decisions or social situations or a constant sense of being overwhelmed. This is your anxiety talking and taking over. Notice it, label it: "My anxiety is kicking up, my anxious mind is taking over." By noticing and labeling, clients are engaging their prefrontal cortex, stepping back from their anxiety, and gaining perspective, rather than going on autopilot and getting lost in the weeds of thoughts and emotions.

But anxiety is like a runaway horse, going where it wants, with the rider barely holding on. Clients with anxiety are often doing exactly that—holding on and letting their anxiety (and energized amygdala) take them into the woods of websites, worries, and disastrous parties. But quickly clients need to learn that they can't continue to do this. Allowing anxiety to run amok feeds the monster—their amygdala will only grow stronger, their prefrontal cortex will grow weaker, and their worlds will become ever smaller. Ellen who used to be able to stop surfing at 3 hours will wind up spending 6, or find her anxious indecision bleeding over, causing her to second-guess herself on ever smaller decisions. By caving in to his anxiety about the party and leaving early or not going at all, Tom will feel relief, but when the next social event comes around—an upcoming date or an invitation to attend a football game—he'll skip the anguish and decide to stay home at the start. And for Terese, not only will the stack of worries multiply, but Klonopin will become a steady part of her daily routine. The way out of this downward spiral, we say to clients, is to stop listening to the dictates of anxiety.

Noticing and labeling when the horse is beginning to run is the first step, but the next is equally important. Clients need to not just hold on for dear life; they should pull on the reins and begin to take control of the horse, and for that they need to know what to do.

Taking Control: Tools and Techniques

Like other CBT-based approaches to anxiety, the Boot Camp approach teaches clients, within the first two sessions, tools and techniques that they can use when they recognize that their anxious mind is taking over and running away. Having a repertoire of tools and techniques helps clients feel less defenseless, more empowered. By having something to do, they are grabbing the reins, breaking the anxiety pattern, and in turn lowering their anxiety threshold.

There are two types of tools and techniques: first aid tools that clients can use when their anxiety rises and longer-term, lifestyle tools that help lower their anxiety threshold overall. Here are some of the common techniques and tools that are offered to clients:

Deep breathing. Deep breathing is the first of a trio of standard and interrelated anti-anxiety first aid—simple, portable, no tools required. While some practitioners spend time in sessions teaching clients and practicing with them ways of counting while breathing, holding breaths, and using the diaphragm to breathe, this isn't necessary and for some clients it often only makes things worse. It gives the impression that this technique is complicated, that there is a right way to breathe, giving already anxious and often perfectionistic clients only more to worry about. Instead, simply demonstrate taking several slow deep breaths and ask clients to do them along with you.

Mindfulness. Actually, deep breathing is a specific form of mindfulness. Mindfulness in general, like deep breathing, is simple and portable. At the first signal of anxiety feel your feet on the floor or your hands on the steering wheel; listen to the tick of a clock, the clank of silverware on a plate. The more senses the better. When you are acutely aware of the present, you are no longer drifting toward the worry world of the future.

This too you can have clients practice in the session. Ask them to begin to ruminate and then ask them to shift focus to the room—have them hear the clock, feel their breathing, notice the colors of the chair, the weight of their hand on their knee. Do this several times so they can more rapidly make the shift and see the results.

Thought-stopping. This is the third first aid standard technique. Just as breathing is a form of mindfulness, mindfulness is a form of thought-stopping. As soon as clients notice that their anxious mind is beginning to run, they are to say, "Stop!" to themselves and shift focus to something else—again, their breath, the sound of the clock. Clients like Terese who may start to feel a flutter of anxiety while driving can say, "Stop," then read aloud the license plate numbers of the car in front of her; when she notices herself fretting over a bill in the mail, she can call out the colors of items in the kitchen. This can be practiced and learned quickly in the session.

However, as Wehrenberg (2008) points out, while clients can learn this mental shifting quickly, they have to be persistent. They will need to do thought-stopping not 10 times a day, but 1,000 times a day at first. In order to speed up this brain rewiring, Boot Camp clients are encouraged to make not just mental shifts but behavioral ones as well. When Ellen finds herself getting pulled into the Internet world, she not only needs to stop the anxious thoughts that tell her that there may be something better; she also needs to get up and do something different—make dinner, mow the lawn, iron a blouse. When Tom finds himself ruminating about the party, he can shift gears and work on his calculus assignment or go grocery shopping with his fraternity brother. When Terese gets that overwhelming shaky feeling, she can vacuum the living room or take the dog for a walk, and do it as mindfully as possible.

The best behavioral distractions are those that can (1) naturally absorb the client's attention, such as Tom's calculus, or something creative, such as playing an instrument, painting, or drawing; (2)

can easily induce mindfulness, as in Ellen's cooking; (3) involve a change of environs, such as going to the grocery store or walking the dog; or (4) involve exercise, such as vacuuming or mowing the lawn. Any combination of these can be used. Clients' particular distractions need to be mapped out with them in the first couple of sessions: "Ellen, what are three things that you can easily do when you find yourself getting lost on the computer?" These are then written down and clients are asked to post them on their refrigerators. Rather than clients having to struggle to develop a plan when their anxious minds have already taken hold, such a ready-made list enables clients to move automatically and quickly to something else.

Emotional freedom technique (EFT). This is an especially effective tool for all types of anxiety: various phobias; mild to moderate posttraumatic stress, such as the anxiety and hypersensitivity following car accidents; situational anxiety, such as Tom's fraternity party or an upcoming job interview; and general anxiety, where clients are encouraged to essentially do a "worry scan"—sit down and think about current anxieties and treat them—once or twice a day to nip nagging worries in the bud.

The technique itself can seem complicated at first (though it is the same series of steps repeated over and over) and so typically about half the second session is devoted to teaching it to clients. It is explained to clients that while this is going to seem a bit strange, it is actually based on principles of Chinese medicine, where problems are seen to reside in the imbalance of one's energy system, and by tapping on the major meridians of the body we are rebalancing the imbalance that anxiety creates. Clients are told that they don't have to believe in the theory, just be willing to try and see if it helps. On the following page is the list of steps that are shown to clients and given to them as a handout to use at home (see Box 3.1).

In order to demonstrate the technique, clients are led through the steps in the session, copying what you do. They are asked to review a particular problem, visualize it like a scene from a movie,

BOX 3.1

USING THE EMOTIONAL FREEDOM TECHNIQUE

1. Think of the problem/situation, visualizing it as though it were a scene from a movie. Make it as clear as possible.
2. As you think about it, rate how strong your feeling is from 1 to 10, with 10 being the highest. If it is below a 6, see if you can tweak the image to make it stronger.
3. Find the sore spot on the left side of your upper chest. While rubbing it, say to yourself, "I deeply and profoundly accept myself with all my problems and limitations." Say this three times.
4. Rate the feelings again. See if they have changed. Don't worry if they have not.
5. Make up a phrase for the problem. Using two fingers, tap on the corner of your eyebrow, under your eye, under your nose, under your lip, under your arm, on your chest (1 inch down, 1 inch over) as you say the phrase each time.
6. If anger is part of the problem, include sequence tapping on the inside tip of your pinky finger. As you tap, finish the sentence "I forgive _____ because _____." You don't have to believe what you say, but do make up some response. Say it three times while tapping.
7. If guilt is part of your problem, tap on the outer side of your index finger. As you tap, finish this sentence and say the completed sentence three times: "I forgive myself because _____."
8. While tapping between your fourth and fifth finger, close your eyes, open your eyes, look down hard left without moving your head, look down hard right, make your eyes go around in circle, go back the other way, hum a tune, count to three, hum again.
9. Think about the problem and rate the feeling again.
10. If it has gone down, repeat the process again. If there is no change: Do a karate chop, the side of one hand against the palm of the other while saying to yourself, "I deeply and profoundly accept myself even though I still have some of this problem with [say the phrase]." Say this three times. If the rating has gone up this probably means that a new problem has replaced the original one. Revisualize the scene, rate it again, and start over.
11. Repeat the entire sequence until you are down to a 1 or 2. While tapping between your fourth and fifth fingers slowly look from floor to ceiling without moving your head. When you get to the top, hold your breath for a few seconds, then relax.

scale it from 1 to 10 in terms of how much it bothers them right now, and then go through the steps, making sure that they hit the right points and tap sufficiently hard enough to feel the pressure. Most clients will notice results right away, reporting a decrease in their anxiety (scaling numbers moving down); some will report having a difficult time imagining the scene. Should the number happen to go up instead of down, it usually indicates a shift in the scene—a new variation of the original problem—and it is treated in the same way.

The worst that will happen is that the procedure won't work, or clients will feel too awkward and have trouble focusing on the process. That's fine; move on to another technique. Clients shouldn't have to worry that they have to do it or be successful. If it works, clients are given the handout of instructions and encouraged to try the technique during the week—for example, pulling off the road and quickly doing the procedure when they begin to feel anxious while driving, doing the procedure before going up on a ladder, going off to the bathroom to tap when they feel anxious at a party, or sitting down and running through the steps when they have a hard time pulling themselves away from the computer. There are plenty of websites and YouTube videos on EFT that clients can check out, and they are encouraged to do so. Looking at these generally reduces clients' resistance by making the procedure more commonplace.

Generally it is found that clients love it and do it, or don't like it and don't do it. That's fine. Your stance is that this is one of several things they can do when anxious: "Try them out; see what you like and what works best for you. Don't become more anxious as a result of the tools themselves." Again, it is having tools, having something to do, that helps reduce the anxiety.

Solve the problem. If Ellen is anxious about what flea medication to use for her dog, she can call up her veterinarian, get a recommendation, and follow it. If Tom is worried about the party but knows he will feel better if he sticks close to his best friend, he can talk to his friend in advance about doing exactly that. If Terese is already fretting about the latest bills, she can ask her husband if they can sit down on Saturday morning and go over them together, or if necessary, bring him into a therapy session so they can come up with a viable plan together.

Clear and decisive action is a powerful antidote to problems and the emotions they stir, but putting problems to rest is a struggle for those with anxiety. Part of the reason is tied to personality, a feature that we'll discuss shortly, which can cause anxious clients to question whether a problem is real or not or inhibit their abilities to act, but part of it is caused by the nature of anxiety itself. The anxiety prevents settling. Ellen may have thought about asking her veterinarian for advice, but if she second-guesses the vet, she's quickly back on the computer following up. Tom could ask his friend to help him out, but if he worries about what his friend will think or assumes that it really won't make any difference and his social gaffes are inevitable, he won't act. If Terese's anxiety tells her that she shouldn't trouble her husband about the bills or causes her to feel so overwhelmed that she can't clearly think of solutions, she'll go back to her default of medication and stay miserably stuck.

Boot Camp clients are encouraged to take action, however small, toward solving problems that are bothering them, rather than fretting about the right action and doing nothing. Again it's a matter of recognizing their state of mind, knowing what's rational and reasonable, and what's irrational and anxiety driven. Here's where you become the reality check and coach for discernment. Yes, you say to Ellen, asking the vet for a recommendation, and maybe even asking why he suggests this one over another, is rational; second-guessing his opinion and spending hours on the Internet following up is the runaway horse. Yes, Tom, talking to your friend is a great idea; doubting that it will make a difference and that your social downfall in inevitable is not. Yes, Terese, letting your husband know what bothers you and asking for help is rational; allowing yourself to stay overwhelmed is not.

As with other aspects of therapy, our voice will hopefully and eventually become part of clients' internal voice. By asking whether there is a problem to solve they are halfway toward solving it;

by taking problem-solving action they are behaviorally reining in the horse. This is what you emphasize, that rather than your getting lost with them in the details of content—the competency of the vet, the world of second opinions, the evidence for social disaster—that their anxious minds generate, they need to focus on process, the doing. The antidote to anxiety is action, and the best action is the one that puts real problems to rest.

Writing the worry list. This is another standard tool: the setting aside of time, generally before bed, to worry for 10 minutes or, better yet, to write the worries down. When this is done before bed, it allows clients to "clear their heads." It also paradoxically allows them to acknowledge their anxiety while having clear control over it—another step toward reining in the horse.

Boot Camp clients are given the homework assignment of not only writing down worries in detail but also noting whether they are rational or irrational worries. If they are rational, clients are encouraged to note the next steps they can concretely take toward solving the problem. This is similar to the writing that clients are instructed to do as part of dialectical behavioral therapy (DBT), where they sort out their emotional mind and "wise" mind. By noting the rational versus irrational, by taking the next step toward action, clients become more aware of their anxious state of mind; this "adult," prefrontal cortex thinking is reinforced, making it easier to label these thoughts as they arise.

Meditation. Solving the problem is both a first aid and a lifestyle tool—taking decisive action when anxiety is rising around a specific problem—as well as an overall approach to problem solving in general as a means of reducing clients' anxiety threshold. Meditation, too, fits into this category, though it relates more to lifestyle than to first aid. Some clients do, in fact, use some form of meditation even for several minutes when they sense their anxiety taking hold. But meditation as part of a daily self-care routine has documented long-term and widespread benefits.

In the Boot Camp approach clients are taught in the same session with EFT the relaxation response developed by Herbert

Benson (Klipper & Benson, 2000). Here are the instructions for meditation:

BOX 3.2

Instructions for Meditation

1. Sit comfortably in a chair, feet flat on the floor. Have a clock visible but no alarm set.
2. Close your eyes and start by taking a deep breath. Just focus on your breathing as you breathe in and breathe out.
3. When you feel ready, begin to say "one" each time you exhale. Continue saying "one" to yourself over and over each time you exhale.
4. If your thoughts wander, simply stop what you are thinking and come back to "one."
5. After 20 minutes, stop saying "one" to yourself and just sit quietly with your eyes closed. If your body feels heavy, slowly begin to move your fingers, your hands. When you are ready, open your eyes.

Additional Verbal Instructions

1. Ideally, clients try two sessions of 20 minutes. If clients are uncomfort–able with 20 minutes, they can start with 10 minutes and work up to 20. Most people find it most difficult to make this a priority.
2. It is best to practice meditation before meals.
3. Do not meditate within 3 hours of bedtime.
4. Clients may fall asleep for the first several days or more of practicing meditation. This is fine; as long as they are sitting and not lying down, they will generally sleep for only about 20 minutes.
5. Clients do not need a quiet place to meditate, but they do need an environment in which they will not be disturbed by others or have to worry about answering phones, doorbells, and so forth.
6. Clients need not worry about finding themselves lost in thought—this is normal. All they need is to bring themselves back to "one," gently, when they realize that their thoughts are wandering.
7. Some days, time will seem to go quickly; other days, slowly. Some days, clients will feel relaxed; other days, restless. That is fine—the meditation is still working and the effects are cumulative.
8. Clients can be encouraged to experiment—saying "one" on their inhale, watching their breaths, simply being mindful of external and internal stimuli. The advantage of saying "one" is that it makes clients feel more grounded and successful.

The saying of "one" to yourself seems easier for many clients than the simple instruction to focus on your breathing. Clients can be guided to do this in the session for 5–10 minutes, depending on time available, and then instructed on how to do this at home. It is emphasized to clients that the effects are cumulative—that it may take a few weeks for their overall anxiety levels to noticeably decrease—and that they need to make time to do this daily for at least 10 minutes, ideally 2 times a day for 20 minutes. Some clients find that this is a useful technique for falling back to sleep when anxiety obsessions are taking hold. Finally, clients are told that the hardest aspect of doing meditation is finding the time to do it and doing it routinely, so they need to make it a priority until it becomes anchored in their lifestyle.

Since this is taught back to back with EFT, clients are encouraged to experiment with both over the course of the week and see what works for them. Some will use EFT for first aid, while others will use brief meditation; some will not like the meditation, and some will not like EFT. That's fine. The goal is proactivity and new skills.

Exercise. Like meditation, exercise helps lower thresholds and, like meditation, it can also be used as first aid. Within the first two sessions, specific exercise options need to mapped out with the client. Some clients already use exercise—walking up and down the hall combined with deep breathing when stressed at work, taking walks in the morning, or working out at the gym after work. Many clients find yoga a wonderful option and they can do it in a class format or on their own at home. Your role is helping them see exercise as a good first aid and preventative strategy and encouraging them to experiment with some form of it.

Appreciating the positive. One of the homework assignments given clients is that of writing down for 5–10 minutes at the end of the day a list of things that occurred that day that were positive. They are told to avoid generalities, such as good health, good partner, lovely kids, a job, and instead focus on the details of the day, as in the cool breeze they noticed when walking to their car, the hot coffee at break, the person who held the door open at the bank.

The goal here is to offset and, over time, rewire the brain from the negativity and tunnel vision that come with anxiety, anger, and depression. Practicing recalling the details of the positive makes it easier to notice the positive in the present, countering the constant future-oriented assuming the worst—the next disaster, the next failure, problem, calamity—of the anxious mind.

Clients can't and don't need to use all these tools and techniques. We are interested in offering them an array of options that they can then begin to experiment with and build on. The goal is to help them find the combination that works for them; by doing so they are not only creating their own unique treatment plan but also taking greater responsibility for their treatment. Further, our à la carte menu sidesteps the potential resistance or performance pressure that might come with prescribing only one or two options. Clients learn to rein in the horse but in their own way.

Link to Personality: Rescuers

Recognizing the anxious state of mind and reining it in with specific tools and techniques relieves symptoms and gives clients a sense of control, but real power will come when they can sever the anxiety from its roots, namely, their childhood coping styles and overall approaches to problems.

As mentioned in Chapter 2, the focus on personality and the core dynamic is where the Boot Camp approach most breaks away from CBT and solution-focused approaches. Here is where we apply the "big six," described in that chapter, and use them as tools for both assessment and treatment. In particular, we can think of anxious clients fitting the profile of the rescuers and victims of the relationship triangle; our longer-range goal is to help them move toward the adult.

It's easy to see how the rescuer role generates anxiety. Being highly sensitive to others and concerned about being good, rescuers not only will notice when their boss fails to say good morning to them, but also will assume that they are in trouble and have somehow wound up in the workplace doghouse, triggering a wave of anxiety. Their overresponsibility for others—I'm happy if you're happy—leads them to overdo things, to worry not only about themselves but also about the problems of others, adding to their worries and stress. The need to please creates an ever present feeling of walking on eggshells, as in Tom's social anxiety around others, just as the need to do what they "should" often spirals into Ellen's perfectionism, that is, a fear of making mistakes, a struggle with decisions (Ellen's endless search online), and an inability to prioritize—deciding which flea medication to buy is just as anxiety provoking as deciding whether to accept that new job. Finally, the running on autopilot of these endless shoulds, plus the fear of confrontation, leads to the stress of unresolved issues and always trying harder, rather than the decisiveness of being assertive.

We look for these patterns, behaviors, and coping styles to identify clients with rescuer personalities, but we avoid wading deep into the past to unearth them. As with the anxiety state of mind, we identify and move into action. We explain to clients that, yes, anxiety is about genetics and brain chemistry, but at a primary psychological level anxiety is about being afraid of the world. From the first session, clients are told that the key to long-term eradication of their anxiety lies in their becoming overall more confident, more assertive, and less afraid and that they can learn to do this by moving toward anxiety, rather than away from it, by stepping outside their comfort zone, and by upgrading their overall approach to problems and relationships. We say to those who display this rescuing personality that this is old childhood wiring, inclining them to be good; it protected them in the past but no longer works, now that they are in the larger world. We want to help them upgrade their mental software, help them become the adult that they are, rather than the frightened child that they often feel themselves to be.

We make sure that clients are on board with this, tracking the process and making certain that they see the connection between their coping style, their anxiety, and the need to take acceptable risks. Here we offer them specific behavioral homework assignments that gradually but steadily help desensitize them to the process of approaching their anxiety and going against their grain, rather than holding on to the runaway horse and following it where it goes. The following are some standard assignments for rescuers.

Shoulds versus wants. This is good first assignment. Clients are to pick a non-workday in the coming week. Before they decide to do anything that day—vacuum the living room, walk the dog, go to the grocery store, watch the football game—they are to ask themselves why they are doing it: because it is on their own internal to-do list, because it is simply what they do, because someone expects them to do it or they worry that others will be upset if they don't, because they want to. They don't need to change what they do, though they can, but just need to notice how they feel.

The purpose of this assignment is to help clients slow down, realize what drives them, and recognize how they feel. Often rescuers find they have a difficult time telling how they feel; they tend to go on autopilot. They are reassured that that is fine; by simply asking themselves the questions they are beginning to rewire their brains.

Notice what they don't like. Being wired to do what they should, rescuers struggle with knowing what they want, but noticing and acting on what they don't want is an important step in discovering what they do. So if their partner suggests going out for Chinese food and they sense a gut reaction that says that they really don't want to, they are encouraged, as an experiment, to act on the gut feeling and speak up. This is framed for them as a two-step process—figure out how you feel, then take the time to figure out how to tell the other person (again, the confrontation, however small, will raise their anxiety). They can take their time, mull it over, regroup emotionally before they step up and be assertive. The point is the effort, not the outcome.

Sometimes even such small steps in assertiveness as this are difficult for rescuers to take with the important people in their lives—partners, parents, supervisors. "Don't worry about it," you say; "practice first with someone who is less threatening: Take the risk of saying no when you don't want to go with your work colleague to Taco Bell, or an acquaintance asks about borrowing your truck; practice is practice." Through concrete actions that move against the grain of personality, clients not only build assertiveness skills but also step out of the martyr role and avoid the buildup of resentment that often leads to internal or external explosions.

And similarly, tell clients that if they ever get a desire for something that they absolutely do want to do—Taco Bell, Chinese food, take the afternoon off and go fishing—to try doing it, not for the food or fishing but to begin to strengthen those gut reactions.

Make decisions quickly. Because anxiety not only requires every decision to be right but also makes every decision seem equally important, clients are urged to practice making quick decisions—buy that latest CD from a favorite band without reading the reviews, or pick out the first flea medication that comes up on the Pet.com website. In other words, act; don't mull and obsess. Let them know that this will feel a bit impulsive and reckless, but that's okay. If they are disappointed—the CD stinks, the flea medication is more expensive—have them push aside that critical voice and instead pat themselves on the back for their risk taking.

Practice deciding who has the problem. If Tom finds himself worrying about whether his friend is having a good time if he hangs out with him at the party, help Tom realize that he is not to be overresponsible for his friend. Yes, he can be sensitive and assertive—Tom can ask the friend who is supporting him at the party if he's okay, but if the friend says yes, Tom should resist second-guessing and doing the spiral of ruminating that his friend is in fact unhappy. Similarly, when rescuers feel that urge to jump in and emotionally bail out people around them—worrying and working hard to help their partner feel better after a hard day at work, offering to drive people home when their car won't start even though it is far out of their way and terribly inconvenient—they need to experiment with holding back, acknowledging the other's emotions, asking how they can help perhaps, but resisting the urge to quell their anxiety by fixing the other's problems.

Again, the goal is to stop going on autopilot and overdoing things and instead to set clearer personal boundaries, and be more adult. Clients need to be warned that these early attempts to go against their grain will trigger anxiety, guilt, or both. That's okay, you say, and expected. Although their critical voice is probably telling them they are in trouble or a bad person, you reassure them that this is old childhood junk, merely a signal that they are breaking out of patterns and taking a step toward rewiring their brains.

Tell others what they need. Because rescuers live with the magical thinking that if they do everything they should, others will somehow automatically know what they need and give it to them, they are left feeling unfulfilled, martyrish, and resentful. As mentioned in Chapter 2, the healing of childhood wounds requires that they give up this wishful thinking and do what they could not do with their parents—that is, tell others close to them directly what they need. Unlike making decisions quickly or saying no to shoulds that are aimed at helping clients act on their instincts and be more spontaneous, here clients are asked to be more deliberative—to think about what they need most from partners, friends, supervisors, and parents and convey it so they can be heard. This may be in a planned conversation with their partner on a Saturday morning, an email to their supervisor, a phone conversation with a friend, or a therapy session to which the other is invited so that they can have support to get their thoughts and feelings out in the open.

Clients will likely need your help with crafting this—thinking through with you what is important, writing down thoughts and going over them with you, role-playing a conversation in a session, choreographing how the session would unfold if the other were to come to it.

Do something scary during the week. The overarching goal of this last assignment and all the others is the same: desensitizing oneself to anxiety and building confidence by confronting fear. This becomes an ongoing task that clients can continue to do beyond the initial sessions. What clients need to be reassured of is that it is doing different rather than doing right that is important. Anything they do that feels scary, they are told, is taking another step toward insulating them from further anxiety.

Link to Personality: Victims

While rescuers are susceptible to accommodation, overresponsibility, and doing too much, victims are susceptible to being overwhelmed, underresponsible, and doing too little. Rather than freezing up under anxiety, they need help toward action, and with practice they acquire greater self-confidence and adult behaviors. Helping them move in that direction requires focusing on several steps:

Reduce the overwhelming feelings. Because the feelings of anxiety become for them not the by-product of problems but the problem itself that overwhelms them, the first step is helping find ways of their calming themselves. Help them label their state of mind in the session—"You seem overwhelmed by this"—and then coach them to deep breathe as a way to relax.

Once you do this in sessions, and once they learn some calming techniques, they can begin to do this at home whenever possible during the week: recognize they are feeling overwhelmed and anxious, label it, and use deep breathing, EFT, and mindfulness to rein in the runaway horse.

Partialize and prioritize problems. The next step is to help them sort and sift through the avalanche—"So you are worried about your daughter and also worried about the bills"—and then help them prioritize, asking, "So which of these is bothering you the most today?" Rather than feeling they are a huge ball of problems, these clients need to see that they are made up of several problems. When they start to become upset, they can practice writing down what they are worried about and then practice prioritizing. They can also make a worry list at the end of the day, numbering the points to indicate which are most pressing.

Take concrete, self-directed action. Like rescuers, victims need to learn to take action to put problems to rest on their own. A plan of action can be mapped out in a session—role-playing a conversation with the daughter, planning to talk to a spouse about the bills. Your skill comes in helping them consider tasks that carry some acceptable risk yet are doable rather than overwhelming. This is often trial and error. Terese may agree to call her daughter and talk about her concerns but then find it too overwhelming to carry out. The assignment needs to be broken down into smaller steps, such as practicing assertiveness skills and building her confidence by having her talk to a co-worker about a minor problem first, or helping her compose an email that she can send her daughter, or choreographing a session where her daughter can come in and they can talk together.

Rebalance relationships. Often victims are engaged in ambivalent relationships with those close to them. The power in the relationship is unbalanced. Victims lean on others when they feel overwhelmed, yet at other times they resent others' control but are afraid to speak up in terms of both possible retaliation and loss of the others as needed support.

This dynamic needs to change. As victims gain experience handling problems on their own and move toward the adult, their dependence on the other decreases. Recalling the rescuers who could not speak up to parents and now need to let others understand what is important to them, victims do the same, with assertive messages that they are willing to do more on their own. But telling others to merely stop what they are doing is never successful; the other person needs to know what to do instead; the old role needs to be replaced by a new one, and it needs to be concrete and clear.

This is what you can help clients define in sessions. Terese, for example, may say to her husband that she knows that he feels frustrated when she begins to worry about the bills. Instead of his just taking over or telling her what bills to pay, she can suggest that they go over them together on Saturday mornings for a few weeks so she can learn how to manage them herself. Assign the homework, then follow up and fine-tune.

By way of summary, let's contrast the rescuer/victim behaviors with those of the adult (see Box 3.3 on following page).

By comparing these lists we can see the direction in which our anxious clients need to go and have the foundation of our treatment plan. But looking more closely, we see that our overall focus is essentially no different with victims and with rescuers: Break patterns; learn to tolerate anxiety, control it, and actively solve the sources of it; heal childhood wounds by taking an adult stance in relationships; build self-confidence through acceptable risk taking. What is different for these two groups are the means. But the overall message is the same: change for change's sake; difference and effort are more important than being right and the outcome.

Transference and Countertransference

Because anxiety is part and parcel of the therapy process itself, particularly in the opening sessions, you often have an opportunity to see the clients' coping styles played out in the room. Rescuers, for example, may easily slip into accommodation, nodding their heads and agreeing with you when they are, in fact, not fully processing what you are saying at all but instead feeling anxious and trying to keep you at bay emotionally. Similarly, victims may easily collapse into a overwhelmed passive role, looking to you for ways to fix their problems, relieve their suffering.

BOX 3.3	
Rescuer / Victim Role	**Adult**
Hypersensitive to others; over-responsible	Sensitive to others; helpful but not controlling
Anxious, feels like walking on eggshells; need to be good, reactive, martyr	Not anxious; sensitive but proactive in behavior; responsible for self
Avoids confrontation	Can be assertive
Difficulty identifying emotions—primarily aware of anxiety	Aware of a range of emotions
Exhibits perfectionism; has critical voice	Has realistic standards; learns from mistakes; can pat self on back
Driven by shoulds	Driven by appropriate responsibility and wants
Becomes overwhelmed by problems, looks to others to take over and make things better	Able to partialize problems and take action to solve them
Periodically becomes resentful / acts out because not appreciated, unfairness	Uses anger as ongoing information about needs and problems that need to be addressed
Has difficulty making decisions / seeing priorities	Realizes not every decision is of equal importance; can trust instincts and make small decisions quickly
Rigid with routines / time; difficulty with transitions; has trouble calming self	Has routines but is flexible; handles transitions appropriately; can self-regulate

Noticing how clients respond to you within the session process helps you quickly identify their core dynamic and role in the triangle. As mentioned in Chapter 2, what you need to be careful of is to not inadvertently foster it. If you sense, for example, that Tom seems to be agreeing with you for agreement's sake, reduce his hypervigilance and "good kid" response by talking softly, being empathetic, giving him room simply to talk rather than struggling to give the right answer—or not only note it but help change it, saying, for example, "Tom, I notice you nodding your head in agreement, but I can't tell how you are feeling; does what I just said make sense to you?" and work gently toward eliciting a honest emotional response.

In working with victims like Terese the danger is that you will take too much control, that their feeling of being overwhelmed will trigger you to save them, take over, tell them what to do. Again, being aware of this danger at the outset can help you not fall into this hole. But you need to monitor yourself and your own anxiety about their helplessness in the session to be able to offer support and guidance, yet enable them to step up and be more responsible. If you have questions about this, get feedback from colleagues or supervisors, from taping or observation, to help you become more sensitive to your own process.

Finally, we've talked about the rescuer and victim positions on the triangle but not the other leg, the persecutors. They are more likely to present with anger management issues rather than the clear anxiety of the other two roles. That said, there is usually anxiety present in those prone to anger and control, and we can think of the anger as a reflection of the same hypervigilance that we see in rescuers. The classic form of this is found in those diagnosed with oppositional defiant disorder. They seem to be constantly belligerent, reactive, and angry, yet underneath they are driven by anxiety and are touchy and aggressive as a way of dealing with a potentially frightening world. We'll talk about dealing with these personalities more fully when we discuss anger.

Now that we have mapped out our framework for treating

anxiety, let's map out the overall Boot Camp goals for that all-important first session.

Hitting the Ground Running: Ensuring First-Session Success

There's an old adage that you only have one opportunity to make a good first impression when meeting someone new, and that certainly applies to therapy as well. Blow the first session by not giving clients at least some portion of what they're expecting and hoping for, and they are not likely to come back. Let's walk through the key elements of a successful first session.

THE INITIAL CONTACT

Actually treatment starts before the first session with the initial contact. Apart from answering client questions about fees, insurance, and the logistics of setting the first appointment, these first conversations provide an opportunity for you to educate the client about the Boot Camp approach. Basically you want to say something like this: "Let me tell you a bit about my approach. I tend not to do long-term treatment, nor do I spend a lot of time exploring your past and childhood as a therapist might do in other approaches. Instead I focus on what is happening now in the present and tend to look at patterns, the ways you approach problems in your life overall. I will give you tools and homework so you can make concrete behavioral changes. It's not just talking about what is going on or why things happened in the past, but instead focusing on helping you change behaviorally what you do. How does that sound to you?"

Most often callers like hearing this: "Yes, this is what I want, concrete tools or things I can do now," or "I've gone back through my childhood enough; I need skills," or more practically, "I can't afford to do long-term therapy. This sounds good." But some may not: "Actually I was looking for something more in depth," or "I feel there are things in my past that I need to reflect on and understand." In those situations, you say that this seems like not a good fit and refer such individuals to someone who offers what they are seeking.

FIRST-SESSION GOALS

They come in. Through your phone call you have already seeded their expectations so that you can start together on the right foot. But now with most clients coming to therapy only once, the pressure is on for you to do it right.

We all know the essential tasks of the opening sessions of any therapy—building rapport and a sense of teamwork, assessing and diagnosing, formulating and offering a preliminary treatment plan. Those of brief therapy are not different, just done in less time. You need to build your foundation within the first session, and there is little wiggle room for mistakes.

Again, as a helpful frame of reference, think of your first session the way a family physician might when you show up in her office with an ailment. Basically you have four interrelated goals to meet in the Boot Camp approach: change the emotional climate, make sure clients feel different when they walk out from how they felt when they walked in; make sure you and a client stay on the same page throughout the session and begin to see yourselves as a team; link the problem to clients' core dynamic and personality to give them a new and deeper perspective on their presenting problem; and leave them with a clear and concrete treatment plan. You can't afford to miss any one of these goals if you are to have a strong start. We'll take them one by one.

Change the emotional climate. There are many ways to help clients feel different over the course of the session. Here is a quick list:

- *Listen and support.* Like any initial session, you need to give time for clients to get out their stories, to be sincerely heard and acknowledged. You want to be sensitive, empathetic. You may match their body position to build rapport or talk with a similar language style. For those who don't have others to listen to them or don't feel safe around them, this can be powerful. Beginning with this helps clients reduce their anxiety and settle; your empathy helps build trust.

- *Take leadership.* But you can't afford to simply listen, nod your head for the entire session, then end with "Thank you for talking today. Same time next week?" All brief therapy is about leadership and being active. You need to ask questions that help you assess the problem and the person, you need to give feedback, and you need to steer the process in directions that you feel are important. Your leadership and "take charge" stance reinforce both the notion that help is coming quickly and that you are competent and know what you are doing.

- *Educate.* This is obviously important in helping clients understand their problems and themselves differently. Just as the doctor helps you understand the relationship between your symptoms and the underlying condition, so does your information about anxiety, tools and techniques, brain physiology, and personality help clients put their problem in a new context. They realize that their problem is common, that it is not their fault, that tried-and-true change is possible.

- *Look for the emotional holes.* In brief therapy one of the best ways of changing the emotional climate is by deliberately creating an emotional experience in the session, and one of the most effective ways of doing this is zeroing in on the session process. You want to pay extremely close attention to the nonverbals in order to tap the subtle feelings that are just below the surface. When Ellen looks hurt, stop the story and focus: "Let me interrupt you for a moment. What just happened? You look like you're feeling sad." If you say this gently, in your best Mr. Rogers voice, Ellen may be able to drop her defenses and actually begin to tear up or even openly weep.

By allowing herself to be vulnerable and finding that you responded graciously and more sensitively than those around her, Ellen will leave feeling different, and she will attribute the change to you and your skill. And even if a client like Ellen seems to push your questions away, you are still letting her know that you notice how she feels and that it's okay to talk about it when she is ready.

Finally, you not only need to sensitively react, but also can act sensitively and proactively by directly asking about the softer emotions that clients are not talking about or showing: "What causes you to feel sad? What worries you the most?" Or ask about positive feelings to offset all the focus on negative ones: "When do you feel your best? What are you most proud of?" Your questions are not aimed at trying to elicit a particular emotion but a different one. You are trying to expand the client's emotional range then and there.

Again these steps may seem basic, but this is where clinicians often fall down. They fail to create this powerful shift. They get too caught up in the story, in gathering history and facts, and they don't notice these emotional subtleties or, perhaps because of their own anxiety, rationalize that it is too soon to tap them. But that is a mistake. Gently go for the emotional jugular, ask the hard questions, and then mop up, again linking your focus and clients' experience to their primary concerns.

Get on the same page. The best salespeople will tell you that the key to closing a sale is making sure you and the customer are in lockstep throughout the conversation. If you miss the frown, if they minimize your strong selling point, you're in trouble. They'll thank you for your time and tell you they'll think about it.

Essentially you too are being a salesperson. Your initial phone discussion has helped orient clients to the Boot Camp approach. Your supportive listening at the beginning of the first session helps them settle down and feel safe. But the most important part of ensuring a successful first session is what we mentioned earlier: *tracking the process like a bloodhound.* This is another place where it is easy to get lazy and fall down. Clients instinctively want to talk about content—their stories, the facts—and again it can be easy to get caught up in it. But you can see what clients usually do not, namely, the process that is unfolding in the room.

This is what you want to focus on and track assiduously. When you make a comment, offer an interpretation, or provide education, watch closely what happens next. Make sure you get the nod of the head, the solid agreement. If you hear a "Yes, but" or a lukewarm "That makes sense" or see a glazing over or a frown, do not move ahead. Stop and fix the problem that is right there in the room: "Hmmm, you're making a face. It sounds like you may see it differently." Gently clarify your thinking, connect your thoughts to clients' biggest concern, and make sure they are in solid agreement with you throughout the session. If they are, and you offer them a treatment plan 30 minutes later, they'll readily agree. But if not, they'll balk, tell you they need to check their schedule before setting another appointment, letting you know then and there that somewhere along the line you fell out of step.

Provide a deeper perspective. Education helps clients see their problem in a new light, of course, but this is where you express your questions regarding what keeps them from solving their problems on their own. It may be situational—they are anxious because they just got fired from their job and are not sure what to do next, or their child was arrested for drugs and they are worried about the legal next steps and about addiction. Normally they can cope, but now there is just too much on their plate. What they need is support, perhaps help with problem partialization.

Or it may be a matter of skill or the lack of it—they have ongoing financial problems because they don't know how to set up a budget properly and are constantly worried or they have unproductive conversations with their partner that all too quickly slide into emotional ditches and leave them perpetually anxious about bringing up problems. Once you help them understand making a budget and implementing it or help them master the keys to good communication so they can engage in productive conversation, the problem fades away.

But this is where you also link their problem to their personality and their core dynamic. You show them the relationship triangle and describe the characteristics of the adult. You map out the steps for helping them upgrade the software—breaking patterns, pushing back and articulating what they need rather than being passive or being good, self-regulating and using their anger as information rather than merely spraying it around the room, stepping forward and taking action rather than withdrawing. This, you say, is how they can update the software and fix not only this problem but potentially future ones as well.

Your zeroing in on this is similar to the physician's talking concretely to you about lifestyle changes—exercise, quitting smoking, eating healthy foods—that not only can reduce this current problem but prevent others as well. Defining and understanding this is empowering. Clients' mental burden of facts, details, and predicaments are reduced to a single primary focus—approaching problems in different and concrete ways.

Offer a clear treatment plan. Finally, like the physician, you need to leave time for providing clients with a clear set of next steps. "This is fixable" is the message. If you decide clients are stuck because of situational stress, such as is common with depression, talk about ways of navigating this challenge in their lives, of concretely solving the problem, of realizing what they can and cannot control. If it is about skills—first aid skills for controlling their anxious mind, for example—outline for them some of the skills you will teach, which they can learn to use. If the plan includes helping them shift from the rescuer or victim roles to those of the adult, outline for them what concrete steps they can take to begin this process.

And then see what happens next. Make sure they agree and are on board. Clear out any emotional obstacles that may block the treatment path. Don't go forward until you feel assured that they are solidly on the same page with you.

These four goals—changing the emotional climate, getting on the same page, linking the problem to personality, offering a concrete treatment plan—give you a map not only of what to do in the initial session but also of mistakes to avoid. Clearly what you don't want to do is (1) *be passive,* as this will prevent you from gathering the information you need and will do little to change the emotional climate; (2) *get lost in content,* because this will prevent you from tracking the process like a bloodhound and making sure you are on the same page with clients; (3) *agree with or merely restate clients' own perspective,* which will fail to help them see how their problem represents a bad solution and part of outdated coping styles; and (4) *fail to offer a clear treatment plan,* for this not only leaves clients feeling disappointed in you and your approach but also gives them the impression of therapy as talking about rather than behaviorally changing patterns.

Treatment Map for Anxiety: Session Process and Content

Now that we have laid down the foundation for the anxiety treatment map, we need to convert this structure into action by mapping the content and process of the opening sessions.

FIRST SESSION: CONTENT AND PROCESS

We can think of the first session as being divided up into three sections. In the first we want to map the terrain of the client's presenting problems. In the second we gather the information we need to develop a hypothesis and, in particular, to identify the core dynamic and how to move the client toward the adult. Finally, in the last section we need to link up Parts 1 and 2 and offer a treatment plan. Here is where we educate, link the problem to personality, and talk about first aid techniques and next steps. All along the way we are closely tracking the process and looking for opportunities to change the emotional climate. Again, let's take each section one by one.

THE OPENING

"How can I help you?" you ask, and Ellen talks about getting lost on the computer; Tom about the upcoming event and his social anxiety; Terese about her nerves, the bills, her dog, and her reliance on medication. Listen, but don't be passive or let this portion of the session run too long—probably 10 minutes is fine.

What do we need to know at this point? Several things, but all revolving around the client's awareness of his or her anxious mind and the ability or inability to override it. We want to know where the client gets stuck.

Here are questions we might ask Ellen; along with the questions are, in parentheses, the rationale behind them:

Can you tell when your searching is overkill and going on too long? (Does she have an awareness of an anxious mind?)

If you are aware, what do you do? (Can she take the reins of the horse?)

Can you ever override your thinking? Even though part of you says you need to keep looking, can your more rational part say that this is ridiculous and stop? If you can do this sometimes, why can't you, do you think, at other times? (Can her rational mind take over? When? Why?)

Do you notice if you are less likely to fall into doing this on days when you feel good versus on days when you are stressed or down? Can you ever tell in advance when you need to be careful so as not to get caught up in this pattern? (Does her anxiety and ability to control ride up and down on her moods and stress? Are there particular triggers that make her more vulnerable?)

Have you had other problems with anxiety? Do you obsess about other things? Do you worry a lot? What about? Have you ever had panic attacks? (Is this situational or more long term and widespread?)

Is there anything your husband can do to help you when you get caught in this anxious loop? (Can family help break the pattern? Does it work?)

Why do you think you struggle with this? (Is her own solution to the problem tied to her theory of the problem?)

Do you take medications? Have you tried therapy before? Was it helpful? How? Have you found things that do help your anxiety—exercise, deep breathing, meditation? (What has worked or not worked to relieve the problem?)

What do you know about anxiety? Have you read books or articles on the Internet? (What information does she have or need?)

What we want to have is a clear understanding of the behavioral pattern, its possible triggers, and her ability to break it. For Tom we would ask similar questions: Does he often struggle with social situations or is this one unique? When and where can he do well, when not? Can he calm himself down and realize that he is overly worrying? Is there anything he can do when he feels particularly anxious that helps (go outside and walk around, sit with a good friend, think ahead of time of stories he could tell)? What is the worst that he imagines will happen in social situations?

Finally, for Terese, the same focus applies. However, while Ellen and Tom are caught up in what they themselves realize is somewhat irrational thinking, much of Terese's anxiety is not irrational; it is grounded in real problems, large and small, that she feels unable to manage. We want to explore her ability or inability to tackle problems head on. Does she talk to her husband about her worry about money? If not, why not? If yes, does it help? Does she talk to her daughter about what is making her angry or to her husband about the dog? Can we help her rein in her anxiety through constructive action?

Our questions help us map the immediate area around the problem. We gauge the client's self-awareness and ability to take action. We have also helped set the pace of the session process—the client quickly sees that we are not simply going to listen and nod our heads but instead interact and gather the information that we need. As we do this we are constantly monitoring the client's reactions. If Tom seems driven to get his story out and a bit exasperated by our comments, we need to acknowledge that we have been interrupting and back off. If Terese begins to seem overwhelmed by our questions, we are seeing her problem replicated in the room and have learned something important about her coping ability; we need to hold back on questions so she can regain her center and feel safe. We are regulating each client's anxiety within the session and, by following the well-known rule that questions tend to raise anxiety while statements tend to lower it, are making constant adjustments all along the way.

MIDDLE PHASE: ASSESSMENT

Following this opening we move to the bulk of our assessment. As with any assessment, what you ask will be determined by your own theoretical models. Here we're using the relationship triangle as our frame. The following are groups of questions based on themes, along with their rationale, which will help us map possible rescuer and victim roles of the relationship triangle and define the core dynamic:

Is there a history of anxiety problems in your parents, relatives? (Genetic disposition, modeling of anxious behaviors.)

Childhood history: Any trauma or abuse? Were your parents strict? Was your family life chaotic? Did your parents have any alcohol or drug problems? (Note: This is not a long discourse. What we are looking for are any remnants of posttraumatic stress, hypervigilance caused by a chaotic or abusive household, overbearing parents who encouraged "good kid" behavior in the rescuer, or controlling parents who undermined the client's ability to become self-confident and assertive.)

What were you like as a child—did you do well in school? Were you quiet, angry? If you had a problem, whom could you talk to about it? (How open was communication, did the child feel safe, or instead was he or she always walking on eggshells and taking care of him- or herself? Again, short answers, not a long exploration.)

If someone close to you is having a hard time, how much does it bother you? What do you do in those situations? (Is the client oversensitive and overresponsible for others—the "I'm happy if you're happy" stance?)

Do you ever feel as if you have to walk on eggshells around others? Do you feel you are sensitive to what others may be thinking of you? (Again, rescuer-type behaviors and hypersensitivity.)

If something bothers you, how easy or hard is it for you to speak up? Do you ever hold on to things and then suddenly blow up over something small? (Rescuer behaviors and periodic moving toward the persecutor role.)

Would you say you are a perfectionist? Do you give yourself a hard time if you don't do as well as you think you should? (Critical voice, high standards, lots of *shoulds*.)

Is it hard for you to make decisions, even at times about small things? Do you worry about making the wrong choices? Do

you sometimes have a hard time knowing what you want?
(Self-criticism and perfectionism, awareness of what we want rather than what we should do.)

What do you do when you get angry? When you feel hurt? When you are worried? When you are sad? (Awareness of other emotions besides anxiety; ability to use anger as information about needs; fear of confrontation; also looking for opportunities to change the emotional climate—"Tell me when the last time was that you felt really hurt or sad.")

Do you have a hard time with sudden changes? Do you tend to map things out far in advance, planning out, for example, your weekend on Monday? Do you tend to follow the same daily and weekly routines? (How well can clients handle transitions? Do they rather rigidly organize their lives as a way of feeling some sense of control and managing anxiety?)

If you start to feel overwhelmed, can you calm yourself down? Do you reach out to others to help you calm down or tell you how to fix the problem? Have you ever cut yourself or used alcohol or drugs to calm down? (Assessing the victim role and ability to take constructive action rather than leaning on others to help fix things or focusing on merely killing the pain.)

Out of everything we've talked about so far, what is it that you are most worried about, that you want to change the most? (Establishing a clear contract and focus for treatment.)

How you present these questions will obviously depend on your own style and may at first blush seem to involve a lot of information to gather. But again most of the answers are designed to be brief, not launching pads into larger, complex issues or history, and again it is up to you to control the content. Think of this as similar to a checklist of symptoms and history questions a physician might ask about various pains or rashes or sleeping problems to complete his or her assessment. We're surveying the signs and symptoms, so to speak, of the rescuer and victim roles and measuring the gap between where they are and where they ideally need to go, that is, toward the adult.

TREATMENT PLAN AND CLOSING

Now that we have fleshed out the terrain of the client and the problem, we are ready to link Parts 1 and 2 and offer the clients, before the end of the session, our preliminary treatment plan and homework. This section consists of four parts: a summary of our clinical impressions and education about anxiety, a map of the overall treatment plan, client reaction, and assigning homework. Again, let's take them one by one.

Summary and education. Work within your style, but here are the important points you want to make:

- *Provide a quick diagnosis.* Say to Ellen that she has an obsessive-compulsive form of anxiety, to Tom that he has social anxiety, to Terese that she has generalized anxiety. If there is a family history, point out that there is a genetic component to their condition.
- *Show the relationship triangle.* This can be a powerful tool in helping clients understand their roles. If Ellen mentioned being a perfectionist, Tom that he constantly feels worried about what others are thinking of him, or Terese that she had abusive and controlling parents, you can point out these characteristics as you talk about roles. Linking them to the relationship triangle normalizes rather than pathologizes their characteristics. By describing the adult, you are setting the stage for making that a part of the treatment plan.

Describe the diagram and the roles, the link to anxiety—feeling overwhelmed by problems and being unable to get them off your plate causes you to always worry and feel anxious; being hypersensitive to what others are thinking of you increases your performance anxiety; being perfectionistic and self-critical makes all decisions equally important and creates constant worry about doing your best. Then ask what fits. Clients will identify themselves quickly. If there is no time to cover this in the session, save it for the next one.

- *Talk about anxiety as a runaway horse.* Here you can mention the role of the amygdala, the shutting down of the prefrontal cortex, and the need to grab the reins and not allow the anxiety to control them and their rational mind.

Presenting a Treatment Map. Talk about treatment being a four-tiered process.

- First, you say, "You need to be aware of when the horse is running away—when your anxious mind is taking over." For Ellen it is when she is getting lost on the computer, for Tom when he finds himself imagining worst-case scenarios about the party, for Terese when she feels totally overwhelmed and shaky.
- Second, you say, "You need to have ways of reining in the horse. There are two parts to this: first aid things you can do when you are upset and practices you can do, such as meditation, that will lower your overall anxiety threshold. I'll be helping you with this. I'll give you first aid techniques that you can use, I'll give you a handout with information, and I'll teach you some skills next week."
- Third, you want to talk about the need for them to decide whether the problem their anxiety is generating is rational or irrational. Wondering about flea medicine, you say,

is rational, but searching for it for 5 hours is not; needing to find ways of feeling more comfortable at a party is rational, but assuming that everyone will see you as a fool is not; talking to your husband about the bills is rational, but getting so overwhelmed by anxiety that you feel that the only thing you can do is take a nap is not. If the problem is irrational, take action to shift the client's mindset—suggest to Ellen that she get up from the computer and cook, Tom can do his calculus assignment, and Terese can vacuum the living room. For that which is rational, do something to solve it—Ellen can call the vet, Tom can ask his friend to sit next to him at the party, and Terese can talk to her husband about the bills. If clients have a hard time sorting this out or struggle to take action, this, you say, is something you will work on with them.

- Finally, you talk about personality, that anxiety is about being afraid in the world, having difficulty trusting others, feeling easily overwhelmed, or feeling that you need to walk on eggshells, doing what you should rather than what you want, being good or making sure that others are happy rather than being assertive and doing more of what you want. Here you talk about ways of coping learned in childhood and the need to upgrade the software to fit the adult world. You can also point out here that anxiety tends to block out other emotions, that often underneath anxiety is some other, stronger emotion—anger or hurt—instead of there being just the worry.

- The longer-range, but important, goal, you say, is "to help you feel less afraid in the world, and the only real way to do that is to build up your self-confidence by running toward what you fear—taking acceptable risks—stepping outside your comfort zone. I want to help you upgrade that software and become more adult (as in the relationship triangle) and help you to use your emotions as information, not walk on eggshells, not get overwhelmed by your emotions, to solve problems as they arise, be assertive and tell others what you need. Again," you say, "it is not that there is something wrong with you, or that you need to do something right, but that you break the patterns that control your life and try to do things differently."

Client reaction. After these words to the client, you say, "Does this make sense?" This is where you watch the process like a bloodhound, looking for a firm yes, a hesitant "Sure, I guess," or a more solid "I understand what you are saying but don't understand . . ." This is the time to eliminate resistance and ensure that there is clarity. Because most clients with anxiety tend to avoid confrontation, they may agree with you, but you need to sniff out any accommodation to your authority. If you are unsure, simply and gently ask, "I know I've just given you a lot to digest. Does what I am saying making sense to you? Is this helpful? Can you see how all these parts tie into your worry about your anxiety?" Again, get a solid yes and pursue any hesitation.

Homework. Doing homework in brief therapy is like doing the exercises a physical therapist gives you for a sore shoulder or taking the medication a physician prescribes at the end of a consultation. The point of homework is to help clients actively change their patterns, learn new skills, and practice taking charge of their anxiety. The purpose in assigning homework is to let clients know that the work of therapy is "out there" in the world they live in every day, that therapy is not *talking about*—using sessions to vent or complain or only get support for their circumstances.

Hopefully, you've covered this ground in your initial phone contact, so it should come as no surprise to the client. If, for some reason, you clinically decide through your assessment that the client is more fragile than you thought, that treatment, in fact, needs to focus on maintaining stability rather than encouraging active change, then, as mentioned earlier, the client is not a good candidate for the Boot Camp approach. You either need to shift to a different model of treatment or transfer the client to another clinician who can provide this type of treatment.

The other purpose, however, of assigning homework is to help you fine-tune the treatment plan. Just as physicians want to know if the medication works in order to verify their diagnosis or physical therapists need to see the results of a week's worth of doing exercises to see what the next step is, you are using the results of homework to not only measure client motivation and compliance but also assess stuck points in the treatment. If Terese, for example, agrees that she needs to talk to her husband about the bills and then she doesn't do so, we need to wonder and ask why. Is she afraid to approach her husband for some reason? Is it too big a step outside her comfort zone? Does she not see how doing this will ultimately reduce her overall anxiety after all?

It's essential to be behaviorally specific about homework, but it's also helpful to be multifocused in assignments. Here you ask what it is that the client wants to focus on most. Getting off the computer, says Ellen, or having some support at the party, says Tom, or doing something about those bills, says Terese. Great, you say, and with Ellen you map out concrete behaviors she can enact during the week if she finds herself getting lost on the computer, or you assign Tom the task of asking his friend to sit next to him at the party, or you help Terese decide on a good time for her to talk to her husband about the bills.

But you also want to include other elements of the treatment—skill building, the upgrading of software. Give clients an article about anxiety management techniques and ask them to read it and try out those that most attract their interest. To help Ellen with her perfectionism, ask her to deliberately make what might seem to her to be mistakes or to lower her standards; to help Tom become more confident, suggest that he try doing anything, especially socially, that feels just a little bit risky; to help Terese better notice and control her state of mind, suggest to her that she check in with herself 10 times a day and see where she is at in terms of her overall anxiety level and think about whether there is a rational problem to fix (but not yet, necessarily).

In receiving a primary and then various secondary assignments, clients have a sense of choice, an opportunity for discovery, and ultimately a sense of empowerment. This attitude that says, "Here are other things you can try," sidesteps the perfectionism that often plagues those who are rescuers; it dissipates the sense of therapist authority implied by "Here is your assignment for the week" and encourages clients like Terese to make choices and begin to take ownership of their problem, rather than wait for someone to give directions and take over. This is, after all, clients' therapy (and you can say this), and therapy is a pragmatic sport. Ultimately we want clients to discover for themselves what not only helps them most but also enables them to run their lives effectively. What they choose to do or not do gives you further information about them, their priorities, and their relationship with you.

Finally, you can close by saying what they often are thinking: "I realize that we covered a lot of ground today and that I gave you a lot of information all at once. Think about it over the week, read the article, and do the assignments we just talked about and see what you notice. Next week, I'll show you some more techniques, but if something comes up during the week that you want to talk about at the next session, that's fine. This is your therapy. I want to cover what you need most."

The message here is that homework is to be attempted, that it is okay to feel a bit overwhelmed by all that was covered in the session, that we will take this step by step, and that the clients' input and agendas (proactivity and empowerment) are important. So off they go with their assignments and hopefully with a sense that they are in good hands.

SECOND SESSION

We have two primary goals in this second session: first, to hear about homework, what was done, what was noticed during the week, so we can begin to fine-tune the treatment plan, and, second, to teach skills, specifically emotional freedom technique (EFT) and meditation. It's good to start off by connecting this session with the previous one: "Again, I realized that we talked about a lot of things last week. Did you have any thoughts after we met?" Here we're listening for solid endorsement—"Yes, that was helpful," or "I found the triangle diagram eye opening," or "I liked the idea of rewiring my brain"—something that tells us that they are motivated, that we are on the same page. Anything less solid needs to be clarified, as in "You say it was helpful, but you sound a bit tentative; are you feeling that way?" and any negative remarks, such as "I really didn't understand how making decisions more quickly can help relieve my anxiety," need to be addressed.

We can see if they have an agenda for the session: "I mentioned using this session to teach you some techniques, but is there something else we need to talk about?" Often no, but this is where Ellen may say she wants to talk about an argument she had with her husband, or Terese may have found out that there is some medical problem that her doctor is particularly concerned about—and this is where you will go. The Boot Camp approach is structured but it is not a forced march.

If they have no agenda, ask about homework: "Did you read the article? Did any of the techniques particularly catch your interest? Did you try any of them out? What did you notice? Were they helpful?" Here we can circle back to the specific assignments we gave last week: Terese talking to her husband about bills, Ellen being able to get off the computer. If they didn't do the homework—"I only read part of the article"; "I didn't talk to my husband"—we want to know why. Not doing it is a bad solution, not the problem.

If they did do the homework, we need to know the results— Terese's conversation with her husband was productive or, no, he just told her not to worry about it and cut the conversation short; Ellen caught herself getting too engrossed online earlier in the week, but on Friday when she was tired she got lost; Tom took a risk by speaking up and saying no when his fraternity brother asked whether he could help out on Saturday, but he didn't get around to talking to his friend about the party. We're looking for where clients get stuck and what keeps them from being successful—what Terese did next to deal with her husband's response, or whether we need to suggest that she invite her husband in to the next session; congrats to Ellen for walking away, checking whether she is aware of the way her stress undermines her ability to override her anxiety; kudos to Tom for taking the risk, but what in particular caused him to not talk to his friend?

Here is where we drill down, find the stuck points, and often tap into the core dynamic: Terese's hesitation with confrontation, Ellen's being reactive and unaware of her own needs, Tom's possible worry about asking for help. We don't need to know the answer; we only need to act on our internal questions and explore what, essentially, kept them from acting as an adult. Their response allows us to reiterate the bigger goals—of working toward approaching anxiety, solving rational problems, being assertive with others, moving away from those perfectionistic standards and critical voices—therapy as the art and process of creative repetition.

Once these situations are deconstructed and clients behaviorally know what to do next time, we can move on to teaching them skills. Again, our goal is to offer a variety and range of techniques—talking about mindfulness with clear and concrete examples, about focusing on breathing, about having several behaviors that can pull the client away from the anxiety obsession, about being assertive in general or taking the time to write down appreciations at the end of the day. We certainly want to be sure that they understand the specific techniques, but we don't want to belabor these—spending 20 minutes, for example, on teaching breathing exercises—as this only reinforces the perfectionistic impulse for rescuers or, for victims like Terese, leaves the impression that here is yet another thing on their plates that they need to worry about. Rather than have clients do it right, we want them to adapt a pragmatic and playful attitude so they can discover for themselves what works best.

We approach teaching EFT and meditation from this same stance, and the rest of the session is devoted to demonstrating these—together taking about 40 minutes. Talk about EFT as the first aid technique, meditation as the longer-term practice. Encourage Ellen to use EFT when she begins to obsess, when Tom feels socially anxious, when Terese begins to feel overwhelmed. Suggest they schedule two sessions of at least 10 minutes of meditation a day. Again provide handouts so they have something to refer to at home and help them practice.

This wraps up the second session.

THIRD SESSION

So far we have laid out the treatment plan and provided the clients with several first aid and longer-term techniques. We have emphasized that they need to work on several levels at once—practicing ways of reining in the anxiety horse but also problem solving problems that have a rational basis and upgrading their childhood coping styles so they are more assertive, more anxiety approaching, more adult. In this third session we are checking in on their use of EFT and meditation, as well as on whether their abilities to recognize their anxious mind, distract themselves, or solve their problems have become stronger.

Again we are fine-tuning, seeing what gets in the way of their being successful. Clients often report liking some techniques more than others. As mentioned earlier, there is often, for example, a split vote over EFT and meditation; some clients find EFT quick and handy even as a daily "anxiety scan" while others find it just a bit too exotic for their tastes and are more comfortable with meditation, even as an impromptu relaxation technique along with deep breathing.

What you will sometimes find here is that some clients are too busy to take the time to practice the techniques even when they acknowledge feeling anxious. They are similar to physical therapy patients who say they have no time to do the exercises even though they are still in pain. We need to question the reluctance—are they not seeing the connection between the assignments and their goals, finding the assignments too great a step either in amount or sense of risk? Again, we don't need to have the answer, but we need to be persistent with the question.

But the busyness itself is often symptomatic of clients' harried lifestyle; they are running on autopilot, putting others' priorities (the overresponsibility of the rescuer) ahead of their own self-care. Just as they struggle to rein in their anxiety, they also struggle to rein in their everyday lives: How you do anything is how you do everything. We need to challenge them on this, show how it is more of the same, namely, old software and a reactive, rather than proactive, stance.

We are fine-tuning other broader skills as well. Ellen may realize, for example, that her perfectionism causes her to be critical of her husband at times because his standards are not as high as hers. We may spend time focusing on specific situations that trigger these reactions in her or briefly explore her ideas about her own critical voice. Armed with techniques, Tom says that he feels more confident at fraternity functions but also realizes that he needs some straight coaching on social skills—how to engage others in conversations, how to listen and ask questions to keep conversations going—and we may educate or role-play in the session a couple of scenarios. Terese may say that she is feeling overwhelmed and confused about her medical issues, and we may help her come up with a list of questions that she wants to ask her doctor at her upcoming appointment. We are hearing and creating variations on the same themes, supporting clients in expanding their skills and coping styles.

Finally, this third session, now that the basics have been covered, is a good time to bring in family and friends as supports.

INVOLVEMENT OF FAMILY AND FRIENDS

It's helpful to state at the start—in the initial phone call, during the first session—that family and friends are always welcome to attend sessions. This seeds the idea early that not only are you flexible and comfortable with seeing others but also family and friends can be an important asset in the treatment. Basically friends and families can help in two ways. The first is as behavioral and emotional support for the client. Ellen can have her husband come in so the three of you can map out together how he can best help her when she starts to obsess. You can quickly choreograph this with Ellen in advance. If she mentions that she would like to bring in her husband next time, take a few minutes just to define what she most wants to talk about, what she most wants to leave with, and what you can most do to help make the session productive.

When the family members or friends come in, welcome them, introduce yourself, and ask if they and clients together have talked about why they were coming here (sometimes they have, sometimes not). Ellen will say to her husband that she wanted to talk with him about ways he can specifically support her when she is anxious. This is a good opportunity to ask about the other's impressions of the client's anxiety—"I'm just wondering . . . since you know Ellen so well, what do you think about her struggle with anxiety?" This not only provides you with a more rounded perspective but also is often illuminating for the client. Ellen hears, for example, just how worried her husband is about her at times, even though he doesn't say so, and this motivates them to work together as a team and her to work on her assignments.

What you then focus on is moving them toward concrete action plans. Ellen needs to say, or the couple needs to decide together, what exactly her husband will do or say that is helpful. Details are important here. Ellen saying that he just needs to "pull me off the computer" isn't clear enough. She needs to articulate what that means: that he will gently remind her, that he will literally physically pull her away or shut the computer off—what? If it is not precise, she's more likely to find his efforts, despite his good intentions, more annoying than helpful, and he'll only feel frustrated or ignored.

The second way of using family and friends in a session is to help the client solve a real-life problem. This is where Terese's husband comes in and they together talk about bills and budget. This is mini-family or couples counseling. Again, your goal is to have them leave by the end of the hour with a concrete plan in place. Be careful as they begin to talk that you don't get caught up in content, such as coaching them on how to best handle the bills, but instead focus on the process, as in supporting Terese in being clear and assertive or helping her husband articulate his own frustrations with her ideas.

Finally, at the end of the session restate what was decided, thank outside participants for coming in, and let them know that you are fine with their coming back whenever the clients would like them to. At the next session with clients, follow up on both the helpfulness of the plan and their experience of the previous session's process. Compliment them on their assertiveness. See if there are any needs for additional family and friends sessions.

Sessions like these can be empowering for clients because, thanks to your support, they are able to go beyond their comfort zone and break long-standing relationship patterns. Doing this in such concrete ways makes treatment more effective and efficient.

FURTHER SESSIONS

What we have mapped out for these three sessions may, of course, take longer, depending on your style or on topics that the client brings up. The goals in these first several sessions are clear and defined. Once the treatment plan is laid out and work is started, further sessions are a matter of keeping clients on track with each of the short- and long-range goals. Each session is about accountability—reporting to you on what works, what doesn't work, what triggered anxiety, how quickly clients were able to rein it in, how much easier it was to implement skills. This is where we track Ellen's overall obsessing, or Tom's overall social skills, or Terese's taking decisive action to solve problems rather than taking Klonopin. This is where you or the client talk about spreading out sessions—every other week, perhaps—to see how well clients are able to continue to move ahead on their own. If you worry that this may seem to a client too big a step, you can supplement every-other-week sessions with accountability phone calls—brief phone messages or 2-minute conversations just for them to touch down and let you know how well they are doing in a given week.

All this is about flexibility and pragmatism, working together with the client to see what helps, what doesn't, what gets better, what is left. Because you are working on core dynamics, clients will often talk about tackling other problems in their lives— Ellen being less critical of her husband over little issues but also more assertive over bigger ones; Tom feeling better socially but now wanting to seek more intimate relationships and feeling yet again a bit unskilled; Terese deciding to quit smoking rather than have the negative effects of the habit be background noise in her worrying about her health. What clients are doing is applying their risk taking, skill building, and changing self-image to broader areas of their lives. Once core patterns are broken, a host of new and healthier ones can be created.

PHOBIAS, PTSD, AND PANIC DISORDER

We have been illustrating the Boot Camp approach with the obsessiveness of Ellen, the social anxiety of Tom, the generalized anxiety of Terese. But what about phobias, PTSD, and panic disorder?

All these often respond well to EFT. EFT can be demonstrated by having clients imagine enacting the behavior that causes their phobia, such as climbing up a high ladder or seeing a spider, and seeing if the procedure in the session helps reduce the anxiety. Clients then can do the same thing as homework—try climbing the ladder or seeking out the spider—to both increase their confidence in the technique and eliminate the phobia. Again the beauty of this is that clients can do this on their own, apply it to a vast array of situations, and have a sense of control.

That said, some clients need some form of exposure therapy.

Here is where family and friends can be brought in as supports, as clients take planned steps toward confronting their phobias. Some of these can be done in the session. Public-speaking phobias, for example, can be acted out in the office, with work colleagues serving as the audience. The goal is the same as in most other anxiety disorders—approaching what you fear through small steps and enough support.

Mild to moderate PTSD also does well with EFT. Car accident victims who are hypervigilant about driving are excellent candidates for this approach. Again, demonstrate it in the office and then ask clients to apply it in real life, while they are driving during the week. Often these situations can be cleared up in a couple of sessions. Clients with more complicated PTSD—veterans with war trauma, for example—may respond well, but often there is a complex of emotions and grief involved and these require a longer-term approach.

Finally, those troubled by panic disorder can use EFT as first aid but also need additional tools. Panic disorder lives on because of the fear of further panic attacks, and this fear in turn gives anxiety free rein. Clients become afraid to go to the grocery store or to church, where there are a lot of people, for fear of triggering a panic attack, and hence they stay at home. The anxiety tightens its grip and their worlds become increasingly smaller. As with clients with the other forms of anxiety, these clients need to go against the grain of restriction and move forward. What helps is support from family, friends, or even the therapist initially in those threatening environments, as well as developing and using an active repertoire of first aid and longer-term anxiety-reduction techniques.

With experience and acceptable risk taking, clients become adept at sensing when anxiety is rising, and this is good. Rather than experiencing a gnawing worry that a panic attack will arise out of nowhere, they can monitor their anxiety level and take remedial action at low levels. Rather than feeling that they are at the blind mercy of their anxiety, clients, through this ability to be proactive, gain a sense of control, which, in turn, helps break the downward spiral and prevents further attacks. Success builds on success.

ANXIETY AND MEDICATION

We've said little about medication and anxiety. Some clients, like Terese, enter therapy currently using medication but are looking for other therapeutic options because the medication isn't working or has side effects that they don't like or because of concerns held by them or their doctor about dependence. Others are staunchly antimedication and come seeking other options. Still others are ambivalent, willing to consider medication if other therapeutic options do not seem to them to be solidly effective.

Since they are coming for therapy rather than seeing a physician for medication, their intentions seem clear, but it's a good idea to discuss their views in the first session. Within a few sessions you and they can tell if the techniques and assignments are working and whether achieving the level they want is simply a matter of continued practice and fine-tuning. Some clients are willing to explore this option at the start, and often just having the prescription or even carrying around a pill in their pocket has a placebo effect of helping them relax in situations. Other times the medication, even on a short-term or as-needed basis, can help break the downward cycle and make therapy more productive; clients' anxiety is reduced enough to allow them to step back and recognize their anxious state of mind and begin to act to rein it in.

Finally, for those clients who have struggled with anxiety for years and have become somewhat habituated to those feelings, they often lack any real sense of what it is like not to be anxious and thus don't really know what is possible for them to achieve. Medication can do this, help them discover what not being anxious actually feels like. Even if they decide not to stay on medication, they viscerally can gauge what it is they are seeking through the practice of short- and long-term techniques. This is often invaluable.

So bring the topic up, refer them to their physician for a consult, and be ready to coordinate with the physician around her and your own treatment ideas.

To bring all of this together, here is summary of our Boot Camp approach to anxiety.

Treatment Map For Anxiety

OVERALL TREATMENT GOALS AND TASKS

- Recognize the anxious state of mind
- Take control/self-regulate: tools and techniques (breathing, EFT, meditation, journaling, among others)
- Increase emotional flexibility and range; discover emotions beneath anxiety
- Determine if there is a problem to fix—if yes, take action on problem; if no, move to self-regulation, mindfulness, distraction
- Link to personality: Upgrade childhood coping; take acceptable risks, define wants; partialize and solve problems; move toward adult

SESSION 1 • GOALS AND TASKS

- Assess: Determine types (e.g., generalized, OCD, phobias, panic disorders); identify triggers, ability to recognize state of mind; ability to self-regulate; rescuer/victim roles; use of medication; personal/family history
- Change emotional climate (focus on soft emotions, education, leadership, listen and support)
- Educate: anxiety as runaway horse; as response to other emotions; define rational versus irrational problems; link problem to personality (show relationship triangle, identify rescuer/victim roles vs. adult)
- Present treatment plan; recognize state of mind; self-regulate; act on rational problems; take acceptable risks; do opposite of coping style

- Get on same page (track process like a bloodhound)—making sure clients understand link between plan and anxiety
- Assign homework: Check in on state of mind; be aware of shoulds and wants; make decisions quickly; look for underlying emotions

SESSION 2 • GOALS AND TASKS
- Give feedback on homework
- Teach EFT, meditation, other self-regulation techniques
- Plan agenda for family/friend session if applicable
- Homework: Practice techniques; experiment with acceptable risk taking

SESSION 3 • GOALS AND TASKS
- Feedback on homework
- Family/friends: Discuss others who can provide support when client is anxious; discuss/solve concrete problems
- Fine-tune treatment plan: Determine where client is stuck—assignments too big; need to develop skills; need medication to break cycle; something else?—explore

FURTHER SESSIONS
- Assign homework
- Focus on ability to self-regulate, take risks, be assertive, partialize and solve problems
- Accountability—use sessions to help clients stay on track
- Determine what additional supports are needed for success

This concludes our discussion of anxiety and the essential focus of the treatment goals, content, and process. We'll use the same framework as a template for the two other disorders. We are ready to move on to anxiety's cousin, anger.

CHAPTER FOUR

Treatment Map for Anger

ROGER SAYS THAT HE AND HIS WIFE, KELLY, get along great . . . except. About every 6 months, it seems, they have an argument that rapidly turns into World War III. And Roger admits that he's the one who invariably ramps it up. Once the dust settles, he's left feeling guilty and apologetic, and his wife stays depressed for weeks. Then they go back to normal . . . until 6 months later.

Sara comes in because her husband, Frank, is threatening divorce, largely because of Sara's spending sprees. While they are able to stay on budget for weeks at a time, periodically Sara goes online and orders hundreds of dollars worth of clothes, which she admits she really doesn't need. When Frank eventually finds out about them, he essentially scolds her. Sara promises to do better and does for a little while, but then always does it again. Frank is fed up; Sara is frightened.

Marie has been written up at work. Her supervisor has been receiving one too many complaints from Marie's staff about the way she treats them—her snapping at them and her flare-ups and bullying behavior—and hearing about the sense of dread that everyone in the department feels. In Marie's mind she is just doing her job, being tough, making sure everyone is getting done what she thinks they need to.

Brett was ordered into therapy as a result of his assault charge. While driving his truck on a secondary road one Saturday morning, he suddenly found himself caught up in the middle of a bicycle race. Not only was he stuck in traffic but a bicyclist accidently hit his side view mirror. Brett lost it. He pulled the guy off his bike and smashed him against his truck. While acknowledging that he had been frustrated, he says he has no idea why he reacted so strongly. He mentions, almost as an aside, that his wife said she has noticed how much more irritable he has been in the past year, ever since his father died.

Once again we have a selection of different faces, this time of anger. As mentioned earlier, anxiety, anger, and depression all easily morph one into the other, but it is anger that is the one of the three that is never what it seems. It is truly the case of a bad solution to another problem. Echoing what we did in Chapter 3, on anxiety, we will look at some of the common sources of anger, discuss the overall treatment goals, and then walk through the crucial opening sessions.

Boot Camp Approach to Anger

Roger, Sara, Marie, and Brett are each showing not only different sides of anger but also different sources. If we look back on our relationship triangle and its three roles, we can begin to see how anger becomes part and parcel of the anger dynamic.

RESCUERS, VICTIMS, AND ANGER

What is curious about Roger's story is the 6-month time frame, the way his relationship seems to go well and then the sudden explosion, signs of an intermittent explosive disorder. In his initial presentation Roger is quiet, mild mannered, and attentive to the therapist. He talks about his work as a manager, describing his supervisory style as laid back, but admitting also that he has a lot of stress, constantly worrying about the performance of both himself and his staff. He works overtime and admits to being something of a perfectionist and critical of his own mistakes. He feels that there are a few on his team who aren't as diligent as he would like, but he says little about it. In general, he says, he has a difficult time with confrontation. At home his wife handles most of the parenting and day-to-day operation of the household and family, though Roger sees himself as helping out a lot with chores and children. When particularly stressed he tends to pull away, withdrawing into his home office.

In his talking about home and work life, you notice that he says "should" a lot—he should do this, should do that—and when asked what he wants for himself in the years ahead he seems a bit stumped. When asked what he does when he gets angry in general, he seems stumped again. He doesn't really get angry, he says, except, of course, when he has these explosions with his wife.

Roger shows many of the characteristics of a rescuer—the anxiety, the performance pressure, the shoulds, the trouble with confrontation. The dynamic of the triangle helps us quickly understand what may be happening to Roger. Like most rescuers, under stress he gets good and under more stress gets even "gooder"—works even harder to make everyone happy. But there's resentment, that others aren't working as hard as he is, aren't doing what he thinks they should, that he is not being appreciated for all he does. But the resentment stays underground or at best is pushed to the side, until he gets completely fed up or overly stressed and his defenses collapse. Then all the built-up resentment gets dumped on his wife, triggered by the smallest of issues—dirty dishes, laundry, the messiness of his son's room. Finally, like most rescuers, he winds up feeling awful about his behavior, quickly wants to get it all behind him, makes up, and goes back to "normal." Whatever problems fueled the argument, whether at home or on the job, are never addressed. Like most issues, they are merely swept under the rug.

But rescuers are not the only ones prone to such explosions. Victims can fall into a similar pattern. Sara says she has always been an anxious person and from the start relied on her husband,

Frank, to take over and solve problems when she felt particularly stressed. This pattern is now solidified in their relationship. But while this works most of the time, Sara, like Roger, periodically feels resentful. Frank's help at times seems to her to be controlling and a form of micromanaging and, like Roger, she gets fed up. She doesn't explode, as he does, but instead goes on online shopping sprees behind Frank's back and each time feels justified in doing so. When Frank finds out, she pleads stupidity or lack of willpower and promises never to do it again. Like Roger, however, Sara too ignores the problems underneath. The way she feels about her husband's control is never openly addressed and put to rest.

What Roger and Sara have in common is the imbalance of power within the relationship that creates resentment, little awareness of their everyday emotions, fear of confrontation, and acting out rather than solving problems like adults.

PERSECUTORS AND ANGER

Marie is dealing with something different. Unlike in the case of Roger or Sara, for Marie control and anger seem to drive her everyday behavior. She is not afraid of confrontation and, in fact, is a persecutor who aggressively mistreats those around her, bullies and uses aggression, rationalizes her behavior, and tends to blame others for making her react the way she does.

Those who fall into the persecutor role tend to be one of two types. Some are sociopathic—they feel entitled, lack conscience, see others as objects rather than people, and are manipulative. Often they have a history of attachment disorder and early trauma. Individuals like these are unlikely to voluntarily seek therapy and, because their worldview is so deeply ingrained, are not good candidates for a brief approach. Many with clear antisocial behaviors will wind up in prison, where the consequences of their behaviors and the tight structure can sometimes begin to shape their behaviors in a more positive direction.

This is not Marie. She is a good mother, albeit a strict one. She can nurture her children, showing a genuine softer side that is not the result of a manipulative ploy. Outside of work, when she is relaxed, her aggressive stance seems to fall away (though her friends would still describe her as a tough, no-nonsense, speak-your-mind woman). What drives her is not a sense of entitlement that announces, "I do what I want," and "Take care of me," but an underlying anxiety. Her controlling behavior is her way of dealing with the anxiety that is always bubbling underneath. By keeping her staff on a short leash, micromanaging what they do, and knowing what is going on all the time, she is attempting to contain her anxiety. And when she becomes aggressive, it is a sign that her stress and anxiety are both ramping up. She is hypervigilant.

As mentioned in Chapter 3, this is what we see in teens and adults diagnosed with oppositional defiant disorder. They are "touchy"; they flare up easily; they are extremely overreactive. Their core dynamic, their childhood way of coping, was one of being constantly on guard and externally focused. Most grew up in chaotic, tense family environments (alcoholism or untreated bipolar disorder in families is the classic cause of this) where there was never stability and safety. Sometimes there was abuse or terrible arguments or fights. And as the research shows, they became wired, as a means of survival, to be ever alert (is Dad drinking; is Mom in a bad mood?) and learned to always be prepared to expect the worst (Child Welfare Information Gateway, 2009). They easily identify with the aggressor in the family.

And like those of the rest of us, their childhood coping styles have followed them into adulthood, even though conditions have changed and the coping software is now outdated and inflexible. Marie, wired to constantly think in terms of worst-case scenarios, finds that it doesn't take much for her to get triggered and once again feel like a threatened 10-year-old. A staff person fails to turn in her paperwork on time or shows up late for work again and Marie's emotional buttons are pushed. She gets rattled, her anxiety kicks up, and she overreacts and blasts the person for screwing up.

Not surprisingly, transitions for such folks are difficult as well. Should Marie's boss suddenly change office procedures, or should her son unexpectedly be sick and need to stay home from school, Marie can once again get rattled. With her anxiety driving her to always think about and plan into the future, it is the suddenness that both disrupts her plans and emotionally throws her off, causing her to get irritable and angry. But like Roger, she is not aware of her own emotions, and she lacks emotional flexibility. All her emotions and anxiety are translated into irritability and anger. She also, unlike Roger, fails to take responsibility for her reactions. She is liable to mutter under her breath about her boss and his ineptness or scold her son for getting sick and ruining her day.

ANGER AND LOSS

Finally we come to Brett. In his presentation during his first therapy session, Brett displayed many of Roger's qualities. He seemed mild mannered, was conscientious on his job and at home, and was somewhat should-driven and self-critical. But unlike Roger, Brett was assertive with his wife and with his supervisor, reporting that he recently approached the supervisor over what Brett felt was unfair about the current work schedule. When asked about his own view about his attack on the cyclist, he said he didn't know what happened; he just "lost it" and felt an out-of-control rage. Unlike Marie, he quickly realized that his behavior was out of line and took responsibility for his actions, even apologizing to the cyclist in court.

When asked about his reaction to his wife's comment that he had seemed more irritable since his father died, he said that looking back, that was probably true, though he hadn't noticed it day to day himself. When asked how he had reacted to his father's death, he said, "Not much." His mother was emotionally falling apart, and as the only child he had to arrange for the funeral. In addition he was executor of the estate, so after putting his father to rest, he quickly had to tie up all the loose ends and financial responsibilities that had come with the role, as well as continue to monitor and support his mother: "I simply marched ahead and did what I had to do."

Brett became the good tin soldier, strong and brave for everyone around him. There was little time and emotional space for him to focus on himself, his own emotions, his own grief. So he didn't grieve—no crying, no reflecting, no nothing. And the grief went underground, coming out as the irritability that his wife noticed. His reaction is similar to what we see in a lot of men suffering from depression. Unlike many women who experience depression as an unbearable sadness and crying, many depressed men sharing the same inner hopelessness become agitated. Similar to the dynamic of Roger and Sara, Brett's unresolved grief continued to build beneath the surface until it finally exploded in anger. For someone else the result might be having an affair, or going on a drinking binge, or shoplifting, or suddenly quitting a job.

What we see in each of these cases is anger as an outcome of other problems—a reaction to stress and overresponsibility, to ongoing anxiety and control, to loss and unresolved grief. We see in each case limited emotional awareness and emotional range. We can ask ourselves again the same question we asked earlier—"What would an adult do?"—and we absolutely know the answer. Roger would confront his employees, be less of a perfectionist, recognize when his stress and resentment were getting the best of him. Someone like Sara would be able to step up and manage her feelings of being overwhelmed, not by leaning on her husband but by solving her problems more independently and if she did feel her husband was too micromanaging, she would speak up and tell him how she felt. Marie would be a leader rather than a bully, not blaming others for her reactions; she would be proactive and clear, be able to set boundaries reasonably and sensitively when the situation demanded it, and take changes in stride. And finally, Brett would slow down enough to grieve, or ask for help, or realize that in his marching forward something of himself had been left behind.

TREATMENT GOALS FOR ANGER

Our goals for treating anger are similar to those for anxiety: a combination of awareness, regulation, and longer-term changes in the core dynamic.

Recognize the angry state of mind. Just as we encouraged anxious clients to recognize when their anxious mind is taking over (the runaway horse), those prone to anger need to recognize when anger is taking over. And like anxiety the goal is to not get lost in the content of the thoughts, but to simply label it: "My angry mind is taking over."

But also as in anxiety it is important to catch this as quickly as possible, and that is often difficult for angry clients. Many report going from 0 to 60 within nanoseconds. We need to help them cultivate this awareness. One simple homework assignment is to ask them to check in with themselves 10 times a day and just ask themselves the level of their irritability: "On a scale of 1 to 10 how I am doing?" They are also asked to notice where the anger resides—in angry thoughts, in blaming others, in tense muscles, in gut-churning aggravation? Are there any particular triggers that they need to stay alert to—being tired and feeling assaulted by problems when they get home, when meeting with their supervisor whom they don't like, having to deal with changes with little notice? What are the signs and symptoms that let them know when anger is or is likely to build?

Put out the fire: tools and techniques. Recognition is the first step; doing something to self-regulate and calm down is the next. Here we can teach clients many of the tools and techniques that we used for anxiety: EFT, deep breathing, writing down thoughts and feelings, exercise, distraction, mindfulness.

What needs to be stressed here is being adult and self-responsible, recognizing anger but not spraying it all over others. When Roger begins to realize that he is upset and starting to yell at his wife, he needs to call a halt, withdraw, and go to a quiet place to calm himself down. When Sara finds herself trolling online for clothes, she needs to stop, ask herself what is going on emotionally right now, and move away from the computer. When Marie realizes that she is already at a 5 on her irritability scale, she needs to sit in her office and not interact with staff until she is more calm, to reduce the risk of unfairly and unprofessionally dumping her anger on them. And when Brett sat fuming in his truck he needed to jack up the radio and sing along or deep breathe and focus on feeling his hands on the steering wheel.

Use anger as information: Solve the problem. This is where a lot of anger management courses come up short. While they do a good job of helping individuals track their triggers and be aware of rising tension, the message that participants often walk away with is that they need to learn to put a cork in it and stay calm.

But there is another side of this equation. Just as it is important for those with anxiety to put it to rest by solving their real-world problems, those struggling with anger need to learn to use their anger as information about what they need. Roger's bursts of resentment are the result of an accumulating imbalance and unfairness in his relationship with his wife and work life. His anger is telling him about what he needs—that he do more of what he wants and less of what he should, that he deal more effectively with staff who are underperforming, that his wife show more appreciation for what he does to help around the house.

Sara has the same challenge. Instead of acting out, patching up, and ignoring the underlying problems, namely, both her dependence on Frank and her resentment of his control, she needs to tackle both—help him understand how she feels and develop the tools to be less anxious and more independent.

Similarly, Marie's behaviors may be a result of her state of hypervigilance, but within her flare-ups may lie problems to be solved. If she is feeling overworked, for example, she may need to delegate more of her responsibilities to her staff *and* provide them with specific training so she can begin to feel confident that they can do the work; or like Roger she needs to have a calm yet clear conversation with one of her employees, rather than snapping and criticizing but not defining a concrete action plan. Self-awareness and emotional regulation are responsible first steps, but solving problems can cut the anger off at its situational roots.

Increase emotional range. Just as anxiety can serve as a cover or blanket for other emotions, so can anger. Those prone to anger tend to restrict their emotions to the one note of anger: They are frustrated and they get angry; they are anxious and they get angry; they are sad and they get angry; they are worried and they get angry; and so on. There are two problems with this. One is that they are missing the information that comes from feeling and identifying underlying emotions like worry or sadness. Instead, such emotions get lost in the mix in their typical state of irritability. The other problem is that others develop a distorted view of these angry individuals: Tom is always irritable; Wendy is always in a lousy mood. Not only do other people have to find ways to defend themselves—pulling back, walking on eggshells—but their one-dimensional view undermines closeness and intimacy, increases isolation, and fuels a "me against the world" stance and more irritation and anger.

The homework exercise to monitor irritability levels can be expanded to increase awareness of underlying emotions. "Check in with yourself 10 times a day," you say, "and on a scale of 1 to 10 rate how irritable or angry you are. The next step when you notice some irritability, at a 4, say, or 5, ask yourself, 'What else am I feeling—worried, sad, scared, hungry, tired, lonely?'" In the first days and even weeks, clients will have a difficult time discerning any other emotions. "That's fine," you say, "even by asking yourself the question you are beginning to rewire your brain." The next step is that if clients actually identify another emotion, in other words, that they are, for example, in fact worried about something, they need to both label the emotion—"I'm worried"—and act on it: do something behaviorally, for example, to reduce the worry, such as talk to their partner or do research on the problem. The labeling and action help ground the emotion, making it easier to discern these emotions next time.

Repairing the core dynamic. Here again we find ourselves in a landscape similar to that familiar to those with anxiety. To ultimately transform anger, we need to link it to clients' roles and coping styles. Roger needs to be more aware of and ultimately dismantle his rescuer traits in order to move toward the adult. We will give him homework to help him separate wants from shoulds, become aware of who has the problem rather than taking overresponsibility, and be assertive with his needs and emotions rather than being good and accommodating of others.

When it comes to Sara, who falls into the victim stance and in contrast to Roger is underresponsible rather than overresponsible, we will work with her to help her take specific action on her own when problems arise, to help her offset her feeling of being overwhelmed and to build her problem-solving skills and increase her self-confidence. We also need to increase her assertiveness, certainly with Frank, but also with others in her life, and we can map out with her a series of acceptable risks to try during the week.

For Marie, our focus needs to be slightly different. We need to first work with her to redefine aggressiveness and control as hypervigilance and anxiety and encourage her to do the same when she is aware that her irritability and control are rising. We need to explain how her persecutor stance absolutely made sense when she was a child in an unsafe environment surrounded by adults who modeled such behaviors, but it no longer fits her current adult world. In addition to helping her regulate her anger and expand her emotional range, we want to challenge and support her in taking the risk of trust. This is where delegating tasks to her staff can be a good initial challenge. Like Roger, and unlike Sara, Marie has the long-term goal of learning to depend on others more, rather than doing everything on her own.

Asking Marie to follow our lead is actually the first step in her reaching this goal: By saying to Marie that the way to unravel her control, aggressiveness, and do-it-herself stance requires that she try doing what she learned long ago not to do, namely, trust and lean on others, we are asking that she trust us. Unlike someone like Roger or Sara, who would be willing to move toward this challenge as a way of being a "good client," we can easily imagine how our request itself can be an emotional obstacle for Marie. The key to overcoming any of her initial resistance lies in our approach.

Not only do we need to make sure she is in agreement with our ideas—that we cognitively connect the dots between her concerns and our proposed solution—but, in order to not trigger her defenses, we need to be extremely supportive and calm in our presentation. Any time her response hardens and her stance gets tougher, we know that we have triggered her defenses and her anxiety. We need to gently acknowledge what we see and nonverbally make it safe in the room for her to relax her guard.

Again, this is where your clinical skill in tracking and shaping the process within the session will come into play. You need to anticipate in advance her possible transference, that is, her suspicion and desire to retain control, and your countertransference, namely, allowing her to have her way or potentially engaging in a power struggle with her about what needs to be done. You need to stay in the adult role, take on the persona of the ideal adult whom she didn't have as a child, who can listen, acknowledge her feelings, yet sensitively advocate for acceptable risk taking and new behaviors.

Finally, we come to Brett. The question here is whether his aggressive behavior is truly situational—driven by the unique circumstances of his father's death and his inability or lack of opportunity to deal with it—or whether it is the tip of the iceberg in his way of coping with significant life events and emotions. We need to ask about his way of coping with other occasions of grief and the management of his anger and anxiety across the wider landscape of his interactions, as well as see if he demonstrates and reports a range of emotions in the session. We are assessing whether he too gets caught up in the dynamics of the triangle or is able to stay more solidly in the adult. If not, we will present a treatment plan to not only help him resolve his grief but also help him up-grade his coping style.

When we lay the treatment map for anger over that of anxiety, we can see the close fit of the two. Both start with an awareness of state of mind—anxiety, anger—bypassing getting lost in thought content; self-regulating with specific short- and long-term tools and techniques; seeing the emotion as information and solving the problem; increasing emotional range; and finally dealing with the core dynamic to move out of dysfunctional roles, toward the adult, and reduce the source of the presenting problem.

Treatment Map for Anger: Session Process and Content

We're ready to move on to incorporating the goals into the session process. Let's walk through the opening sessions.

THE INITIAL CONTACT

Your focus is here the same as with anxiety. You use the initial phone or email contact to quickly determine if the client and his or her problem is appropriate for your practice and style, to answer logistical questions, and to begin to set expectations by briefly defining the Boot Camp approach.

What can be different with clients presenting with anger issues is their own ambivalence or initial resistance. We could imagine Marie saying that she is contacting you because her supervisor wants her to get some counseling, or Brett saying that his attorney suggested he find someone to help make a better case in court or to comply with the court order, or even Roger and Sara saying that they are mainly concerned that their spouses are upset with them and they want to get some counseling as a way of showing their partners that they are sensitive to their concerns.

The problem with each of these scenarios is that the prospective client is not fully owning his or her problem. Each is contacting you only to appease someone else. We're back to discerning who has the problem, and in these scenarios the problem seems to lie with Marie's supervisor, Brett's attorney, Roger's wife, and Sara's husband.

In order to hit the ground running, the client needs to be fully on board, and this initial contact is a good place to make sure of this. If Marie says that her supervisor wants her to get counseling or Brett says that his attorney suggested contacting you, your next question is essentially "And what do you think? It sounds like they think counseling would be helpful, but do you?" Even with Roger we might say something like "It sounds like your wife is worried about your reactions and you are being sensitive to her, but are you worried about your own behavior?" There are basically only four different types of responses to such questions: resistance, unclarity, ambivalence, or agreement.

Resistance. If Marie, for example, says no, she doesn't feel she needs counseling, she is only doing her job and it is her boss who has the problem, you may want to say that this seems to be a personnel issue that she may want to take up first with human resources or her supervisor's supervisor. If Brett says that he is only doing this because he agrees with his attorney that it might help his court case if he were to able to say that he saw a counselor, you might want to explain that you don't feel comfortable providing this type of service, or depending on your style, you may agree to see him once and you both can decide if it might be worthwhile after all. If Roger says that his wife always overreacts to little things, you might say that it seems that he feels as though she actually has the problem and it is she who needs help with it, not he, or that perhaps they would do better to come in as a couple.

Sometimes, however, the resistance you hear is less about who has the problem and more about the notion of therapy itself. For those who have never been in therapy before the process itself can seem mysterious or intimidating and cause them to be less than enthusiastic; those who have had bad therapy experiences in the past can be gun-shy. Others may seem resistant because they are uncertain how therapy can help at all and are unable to link the problem with the process. If I'm having problems with my supervisor, says someone like Marie, how is talking to you about her going to help me get along with her better?

Here, in a general way, you can explain to Marie how therapy can help her communicate more clearly with supervisor, give her strategies for solving work problems, or help her learn new ways of managing her stress. If you suspect that the person may have had poor experiences with therapy, and you have the time to briefly explore this on the phone, do so: "From what you just said, it sounds like the time you saw a counselor it was not a good experience for you. Let me briefly explain how I work and answer some of your questions." If you do not have the time, offer to discuss further on the phone, refer the client to your website, or offer the appointment with the understanding that it is simply an introduction and opportunity to meet and address his or her concerns.

Unclarity. Unclarity refers to the prospective client's not fully understanding the purpose of the referral. Marie says that her supervisor is recommending counseling but she is not sure why; or Brett says that his attorney has suggested sessions but he doesn't really see how it would help him or even his case; or Roger says that his wife thinks he needs counseling, but they have made up, they have put the argument behind them, and in his mind it's over. In these cases either say that they seem unclear about the other's concerns and that it might be a good idea to clarify it with them further before making an appointment or, alternatively, suggest that they come in with the other person—the supervisor, the attorney, the spouse—for a session.

The purpose here is to provide a safe environment and opportunity for the other to express his or her concerns and for you to facilitate the process by asking hard questions—asking Marie's supervisor what her biggest concern is about Marie's work or her team from the supervisor's perspective, or asking the attorney whether she sees any value in counseling for Brett apart from the legal issues, or asking Roger's wife about her overall impressions of their relationship. What you don't want to do is offer to do this work for them—to ask their permission for you to call up the supervisor, attorney, or spouse. Not only are you being overre-sponsible, but you also are caught in the middle—"Your supervi-sor said . . ." and Marie only says that the supervisor is wrong or never said that to her.

Ambivalence. Ambivalence would be expressed as the "I guess"—Marie says that *maybe* she can be a bit abrasive at times, or Brett says that apart from looking good in court, talking to someone *might* be helpful, or Roger or Sara say that yes, their partners tend to overreact but, sure, they could see why they were particularly upset this last time. While their motivation may not be at a full 100% there is something to work with, and you can simply say that you would be happy to schedule an initial appointment to see if you both feel that this can be helpful.

Court-ordered cases often lie at the crossroads of resistance, unclarity, or ambivalence. Some court-ordered clients clearly feel they were wronged by the court, think counseling is not needed or is in general a waste of time, and are willing to come to therapy only to comply with the order and get it done. Others are not clear about the purpose behind the order.

Sam, for example, was ordered into counseling following an assault on his wife. He stated flatly to the therapist in the first session that he didn't need to be there. He presented his version of the problem: He drinks only beer, he related, as he has learned over the years never to mix beer and hard liquor or he "gets cra-zy." Well, his grown son happened to bring over some vodka a few weeks ago and, he admits, he made a mistake, broke his rule, and drank some vodka along with his beer. And as he should have known, he "got crazy" and hit his wife (accidently, in his mind). Anyhow, he says to the therapist, he learned his lesson and since then has gone back to sticking with just beer and he and his wife have been doing just fine. End of story.

In his mind the therapy is unnecessary—the event was in the past; he has his own understanding of the problem; for him it is resolved. But with a bit of prodding, Sam may reveal that he is less closed than he at first seems. Apart from the dangerous beer-and-vodka adventure, he wonders at times if his beer drinking is getting the best of him. Yes, he's willing to talk about that and that's a good enough starting point for treatment.

In all these scenarios your goals are the same—to first define who has the problem and then to help prospective clients understand the connection between their concerns and the therapy process—what it can and cannot do, what the process is like. Because how you do anything is how you do everything, it doesn't matter where you start as long there is an agreement with the client to start somewhere. What you want to avoid is getting caught being both therapist and cop—the enforcer of the court order, for example. The roles are at cross purposes.

If Sam doesn't want to come for therapy, the best you can do is connect the dots and explain how therapy may be helpful. But it is important that you help him leave the session understanding that therapy is not the end but the means, that what is undoubtedly driving the court order is a behavioral bottom line. The judge ordered Sam for counseling because Sam hit his wife, vodka or not; similarly, Brett was ordered to court for attacking a cyclist, whether or not the cyclist should or should not have hit Brett's mirror—and these are unacceptable behaviors that the court does not want repeated. Therapy is considered one way of helping them deal with their reactions. If they don't feel it would be helpful or if they feel they don't have a problem, they need to talk to their lawyer. The court and community doesn't ultimately care whether they come for counseling; what they care about is that they don't produce these behaviors again.

Agreement. Here the client takes responsibility. Yes, Marie's supervisor can be overbearing herself, but Marie realizes that she overreacts to staff at times. Brett is in fact surprised by his own anger and aggression at the cyclist and it concerns him. Roger says that these big arguments may be 6 months apart, but they are World War III and he realizes that it is he who has a difficult time keeping things from escalating. Sara agrees with Frank that her spending habits are a problem. We are good to go.

THE FIRST SESSION

Our goals for the first sessions are the same as those for anxiety, namely, changing the emotional climate, providing a new perspective on the problem, providing a clear treatment plan, and as always making it all work by tightly tracking the process. Let's walk through this first session.

The opening. We start with the story. Roger talks about his argument with his wife, Sara describes her shopping and the pattern in their marital relationship, Marie talks about her discussion with her supervisor and the supervisor's concerns about her treatment of the staff, and Brett talks about the bicycle race and his attack on the cyclist. We listen but ask enough questions to be able to map the sequence of events and emotions: "So, Roger, tell me how the argument started. And what happened next? Could you tell that you were beginning to get upset, that the conversation was going off track?" "Sara, when you decided to look online for clothes, what do you think prompted the idea? Were you aware of how you were feeling? So Frank gets upset, but I'm wondering if you get upset at him sometimes as well." "So, Marie, your supervisor calls you in. Were you surprised by what she said? Did you know what she was referring to? How did you feel about her comments? What did you say back? What she called mistreating staff, what do you call it? Were you able to help her understand your point of view?" "Brett, so how did you feel when you were sitting stuck in traffic? What happened inside you when the guy hit your mirror? What were you thinking or feeling? How did you feel about what you did?"

What we are looking for in these opening questions are two things: level of self-awareness in the moment and ownership of problems and behaviors rather than defensiveness. Roger says he can tell that he was getting upset or was falling into the emotional hole of Christmas 2006 again with his wife but couldn't put on the brakes. Sara says that while Frank does a good job of managing money issues that easily overwhelm her, she also feels at times that he is a bit rigid and controlling. Marie says she was surprised by her supervisor's comments but was able to remain calm in the meeting and did her best to describe her supervisory style, even though she felt angry inside. Brett had no idea what happened— he felt mildly frustrated by being stuck in traffic but then went from 0 to 60 when his mirror was hit. We are beginning to get an initial impression of clients' ability to recognize their state of mind in stressful situations, their ability to self-regulate and control emotions, and most of all their ability to remain adult and take responsibility for themselves rather than blaming.

Finally, our priority at this opening stage of the session is to create safety by remaining relaxed, actively listening, and gently probing to begin to shape the process. We are careful about how we sound. We know in advance that we don't want to sound critical or overbearing like Roger's wife or Marie's supervisor, or aggressive or insensitive like Brett's cyclist. This would only replicate the problem and do little to change the emotional climate.

Assessment. Once the presenting problem and story are on the table we are ready to move to our own assessment—what information we need to formulate our hypothesis and uncover the problem under the client's presenting problem. As in Chapter 3, what follows are typical questions in italics, with the rationale behind the question in parentheses. We'll group them by broad topics.

Self-Regulation

Apart from the situation you described, are there other situations that cause you to get angry? (Is this an isolated incident, such as possibly Brett's, or part of an ongoing pattern?)

Have you noticed any particular triggers, that is, things that you are particularly sensitive to that can cause you to feel angry? (Awareness of triggers—for example, someone doesn't

listen or interrupts me, someone who I feel is talking
down to me, someone who doesn't follow through on
what I ask them to do, etc. Ask follow-up questions to
isolate specific behaviors—for example, what does "talking down to you" mean?)

*How quickly do you go from 0 to 60? Can you tell when you are
beginning to get irritated or frustrated? Can you tell, for example, when you wake up or are coming home from work that
you are in a bad mood and feeling vulnerable?* (Awareness of
angry state of mind)

*Can you tell when your reactions are overreactions even if you
can't always control them?* (Self-awareness)

*Do you tend to feel that it is other people who make you angry,
that, for example, they talk down to you or look at you in a
certain way, causing you to get upset?* (Blaming others for
anger, the ability to take responsibility for emotions)

*If you realize that you have overreacted, do you go back, apolo-
gize, and calmly discuss the problem?* (Ability to be adult,
ability to return and repair, use anger as information and
solve the problem)

*If you begin to get upset, is there something that someone close
to you—your spouse, your friend—can do that would help
you calm down? Is there something this person shouldn't do
that would make it worse? Have you ever told him or her this?*
(Ability to use others for support with emotions)

*Do you have ways that you have discovered do help you calm
yourself, for example, leaving the scene and doing something physical, deep breathing or counting, punching a
pillow or talking yourself down, telling yourself that you are*

overreacting and need to remain calm? (Possession of an arsenal of techniques to self-regulate that work)

Do you use drugs, alcohol? How do they affect your anger? (Self-medication through drugs)

Have you taken medication for anger, anxiety, or depression? Did (does) it help? (Past experience with medication, openness to use)

Emotional Flexibility and Anxiety

What do you do when you feel sad? worried? hurt? scared? depressed? How difficult is it for you to tell when you are feeling these different emotions? What do you do when you notice you are feeling one of these feelings? (Emotional flexibility and range; ability to feel and use other emotions as information)

Can you tell others when you are feeling these other emotions? (Ability to be intimate, trust, use others for support)

Is there one emotion that is particularly hard for you to feel or express? (Emotional holes)

Can you tell when you are feeling anxious? What do you notice most? (Ability to recognize anxiety under the anger, ability to recognize hypervigilance, symptoms of anxiety)

Do you have a difficult time with transitions, for example, when things suddenly turn out differently from what you planned or when your plans are suddenly changed? How do you react? (Underlying anxiety, rigidity, difficulty shifting gears)

Do others see you or do you even see yourself at times as being controlling of others, that is, wanting them to do what you want? (Control as way of coping with underlying anxiety)

Core Dynamics

Why do you think you have a quick temper (or so easily get angry, or have trouble controlling your anger)? (Theory about source of anger)

What were your parents like? Were they strict, laid back? Did you get along with them? Is there any history of physical, emotional, or sexual abuse? (Abuse history; structure vs. chaos; possible identification with the aggressor; possible posttraumatic stress)

If you had to pick one word to describe how it felt to be in your family most of the time, what would it be? (Family climate, anxiety, fear, and hypervigilance)

How did you cope under these situations/this stress? (Childhood coping styles, rescuer, victim, persecutor roles)

When you had a problem, how easy or hard was it for you to talk to your parents about it? Did you talk to anyone else for support? (Trust, ability to reach out)

If you could have any changed any one thing about your family or parents, what would it be? (Determining what had the biggest impact on self)

What was the one thing you needed that you felt you didn't get or get enough of? (Unmet needs)

Did either or both of your parents have problems with anger? What did they do when they got angry? What did you do when they got angry? (Modeling of anger and possible identification with the aggressor; childhood coping style)

Have you had any recent losses? Any major losses in the past? How did you handle them? (Unresolved grief, grief going underground, correlation between unresolved grief and increased irritability)

These may seem to be a lot of questions, but once again we are avoiding lengthy discussions. Like the physician we are essentially moving through a checklist to map holes, self-awareness, roles, and initial diagnosis.

CHANGING THE EMOTIONAL CLIMATE

Making alterations in the emotional climate remains one of our goals for the first session and, as with anxiety, we are looking for opportunities to carry out this goal. One way will come through education, which we'll describe shortly, but the other way, which is particularly important in dealing with anger, is tapping into softer emotions. As clients talk about their story, it's highly possible that in the telling their anger will be ignited. We can imagine Marie getting irritated once again as she describes her relationship with her supervisor, Brett again getting angry that the cyclist hit his mirror, or Roger or Sara feeling upset about their partners. While we want to help them distill the information within the emotion, we also want to flesh out the softer underside, both to gauge their emotional flexibility and range and to help them feel different when they walk out from how they felt when they walked in.

So as we did for anxiety, we are looking for cues in the process. When Roger talks about feeling bad about yelling at his wife and begins to ever so slightly tear up, we ask him gently how he is feeling. When Marie mentions her daughter and how much she enjoys her we ask her to tell us more about her or what she enjoys most about being a mom. Or when Brett mentions his dad we ask what he misses most about him. We ask about fear, asking when Sara mentions divorce and also asking whether she ever feels afraid of Frank when he is upset; when Marie describes her parents and their rages when she was a child, we say that it must have been scary for her to live with such a family.

We're also back to being aware of the nuances of transference and countertransference and mapping out for ourselves how we need to not replicate the problem and help lower defenses. We certainly know we do not want to sound reprimanding like Marie's supervisor or Sara's husband but instead be the patient listener. We view any sign of Roger's "good kid" accommodation as an indication that his defenses are up; we need to be gentle and nonthreatening or move under his defenses by asking what he feels his wife doesn't understand about him most. We need to not condone Brett's aggressive behavior but gently ask about his frustration or listen quietly when he begins to talk about his father, to draw out emotions that he has kept bottled within.

Will we break through defenses each and every time? Probably not. But again this is where your clinical sensitivity and skill most come into play. Through our questions and tone of voice, we are guiding the process, seeding or opening emotional doors, letting clients know what is okay to talk about and encouraging them to take emotional risks.

PROVIDING EDUCATION

As with the treatment of anxiety, providing education is powerful in the treatment of anger because it has the capacity to change the emotional climate while placing the anger in a broader context. Here are key ideas to present:

Show them the relationship triangle. Because so much of anger is sporadic, showing clients the dynamics of the relationship triangle helps explain in a different way the source and reason for their behaviors: "Let me show you something that I show everyone, and then you tell me what fits." Roger has the opportunity to see how he fits into the rescuer role and has an explanation of how his life of overresponsibility and building resentment can lead to his explosions every 6 months. Sara can visually understand how in her relationship with Frank he seems to constantly be in control and how her resentment can lead to persecutor behavior and acting out. Marie may be able to identify herself as moving between the rescuer and persecutor roles, and if you place it in the context of hypervigilance and learned childhood coping style, she can hopefully see her behavior in a new light. Even Brett may find that he is more like Roger than you initially thought, and it is not just the grief but his own accommodation and overresponsibility that fuels his periodic anger.

What they also see and hear, of course, is information about the adult. Here is where Roger, Brett, and Marie can understand how being clear about who has the problem can help them break old relationship patterns. And Sara can see how by learning to take more responsibility in managing her anxiety and problems she can move away from what seems to be Frank's overbearing control. This, you say, is the place you want to help them get to.

Present the model, see their reactions, and say that the fact that there is a diagram describing this means that these dynamics are common. You want to help them see that what they are doing makes sense, that their anger is the outcome, not the cause, of an imbalance. And if they seem hesitant or confused, don't be afraid to state what you believe is going on and see if they too can make the connection.

Educate on the angry state of mind, emotional flexibility, anger as information, anger and grief. Drawing on the information you gathered in your assessment, you want to educate on specific qualities of anger. Here are some things you may want to say:

> What's important in learning to control your anger, and what you seem most concerned about, is having ways of calming yourself down when you are upset. But the real starting point is realizing when what I call your angry mind is taking hold. Sometimes you realize it by how you are talking to yourself and sometimes by a feeling in your gut; sometimes it builds slowly, but often it seems to come on

suddenly and you quickly go from 0 to 60. The more quickly you can realize that your annoyance, irritation, or anger is building, the better. Then you can do things, which I can show you, to help you calm down.

Often people who have difficulty with anger, like those with anxiety, also have a hard time feeling and identifying other emotions, or they can feel anxious or angry but little else. You said that this is true for you, that you have a difficult time knowing when you are sad or scared. Not only do you miss knowing how you are really feeling, but others around you only get one view of you, usually that you seem always irritable or angry.

Yes, it is important that you learn to control your anger so that it does not hurt others, but you don't just want to suppress it. Your anger is telling you something about something that you need and are not getting, about a problem that you need to focus on and solve.

What you are describing I have seen and heard before, where there is a big loss in your life—the death of a parent, a good friend—and you are called on to take charge, to take care of others who are overwhelmed by grief. You become the good tin soldier and your grief gets pushed to the side. Over time it begins to come to the surface, often not as sadness but as irritability and anger.

Talk about the core dynamic and long-term goals. To have the greatest impact it is important to connect the core dynamic and long-term goals to the clients' specific personalities. Here is what you may say to each of our clients:

To Marie: "It sounds like you had a difficult childhood and with the chaos and abuse going on in your family, you had to learn to always stay on guard. It worked for you then, kept you alive, but now it doesn't work as well at your job, where others see you as overreacting and angry. It's time to update the software, to have your reactions better fit your adult life."

To Roger: "You pointed out in the relationship triangle that you see yourself as the rescuer. You learned to cope as a child by being good, by doing what you should, but now the world has got bigger so you easily feel stretched, and, more important, what you want gets lost and leads to resentment. I want to help you do more of what you want and help you tell people what you need, to help you be less overresponsible."

To Sara: "It sounds like you can easily get overwhelmed and didn't have the opportunity in growing up to feel self-confident and handle problems on your own. In your marriage you have relied on Frank to take over when you feel overwhelmed. The problem with that is that you both have fallen into roles that are hard to step out of and periodically you get resentful of Frank's control. What will help you become less resentful is learning to be more self-confident and doing things on your own and relying less on Frank."

To Brett: "It sounds like you never had a chance to grieve your father's death and I want to help you do that. But you are also saying that overall you have a hard time expressing your feelings, that you keep a lot of things inside, and you undoubtedly learned to do this as a child because that's how everyone in your family was or because it wasn't safe for you to show your feelings. I wonder if it would also be helpful to try experimenting with noticing how you feel and also to try sharing these feelings with others so you don't have to continue to bottle them up."

Again, what we are doing through each of these educational points is reframing the presenting problem, as well as changing the emotional climate. Along the way, we are always tracking the process, making sure that we and our clients are on same page, that what we say makes sense to them and helps them see their problem in a new way. If this is not the case, stop and fix the problem: "It sounds like you don't agree." "You are looking confused." "Tell me what you think about what I am saying." Do not move forward unless there is consensus.

PRESENTING THE TREATMENT PLAN

In educating clients in the aspects of anger we have essentially covered all the major elements of treatment: recognizing the angry state of mind, using self-regulation, increasing emotional flexibility and range, using anger as information and solving the problem, and being aware of and changing core dynamics and its childhood coping mechanisms. But ultimately as clinicians we need to ask ourselves, just as we did with anxiety, "What is it that this person needs to do to be more adult?" or stated another way, "What prevents the person from acting more adult?" Here is where we tailor our focus to each client. So by way of summary, let's present our specific treatment plans for each of our four clients.

Roger. Roger, there are several things that I think we need to work on. The first, and the one you seem understandably most concerned about, is having ways of reining in your anger so that it doesn't escalate and cause real wounding to your wife. So we need to help you learn when anger is building and then have ways of calming yourself down.

But the fact that these arguments come on only every few months and with such ferocity suggests to me that they are a result of resentments building up that you don't recognize or are afraid to talk about with Kelly. We need to focus on this. You said you saw yourself as the rescuer, and I agree. You want to pay closer attention to how you are feeling, being able to identify things that you like or don't like, rather than going on autopilot and doing what you feel you should or what will make others happy. When Kelly seems to not appreciate you or is not taking on her share of responsibilities, you need to tell her how you feel. Use your feelings as information so that she has a chance to help fix the problem, give you what you need; the explosions will stop once you solve the problems. It may be helpful to have your wife come here with you so you have a safer place to talk and help her understand how you feel.

Finally, as I mentioned earlier, what you are doing with your wife—taking on a lot of responsibilities, being a martyr at times—is something you learned at an early age and probably what you do in other areas of your life, such as at work. To break out of this role you want to be aware of when you are taking on problems that are not your own, and you will want to move toward more of what you want to do rather than always doing what you should. Finally, you can practice being assertive with others besides your wife; this is actually often a safer place to start. If your supervisor, for example, is doing something that is bothering you or if you are feeling unappreciated, try being assertive and talk about it with him. Yes, this may feel intimidating at first, but what's important is taking the risks of speaking up sooner so resentments don't build.

Does this make sense?

Sara. *I know you are worried about your husband's threats of divorce. Part of the problem here is one of communication; he doesn't understand why you periodically go off budget and go on spending sprees. As I said when I was showing you the relationship triangle—and what you said made sense to you—is that you lean on him a lot to fix problems when you get overwhelmed but also at times resent his seeming micromanaging and control of you. Is this true?*

So we have a few things to work on. One is keeping your resentment from building up and causing you to act out. Here's where you and I or you and I and Frank need to have a discussion about how you feel at times, those times when you feel controlled. If you are not sure when those times are, a good starting point would be to just notice how you feel as you go through the week interacting with him.

It sounds like you also sometimes have a hard time realizing that your anger is building up or even at times connecting it with your shopping. So I'm thinking that we could work on helping you realize when those feelings are building up and having other ways of coping with them before you find yourself wanting to go online and shop. Part of this again is learning to pay attention to how you feel, and part of it is ultimately being able to talk to Frank about it.

But as I mentioned earlier, and you agreed, all these are ways of coping that you have been using for a long time. You learned these as a child as a way of being in your family. Ultimately, I think, you want to have ways of not getting overwhelmed, of dealing with problems on your own rather than turning to Frank. This will help you feel more adult and self-confident and will allow Frank not to feel that he always has to take over. This is a matter of developing skills and practicing them—taking concrete action to solve problems more on your own—and rather than turning things over to Frank, letting him know how he can support you so you can do this yourself. Again, it might be good for Frank to come here with you so you have a safe place to talk with him about this.

Does this make sense?

Marie. I believe I understand that you feel that you are just doing a good job at work and only holding people to the standards that are expected. It also sounds like problems come up at those time when you seem irritable and angry with staff—yes? I think we have a few things that we can work on.

First, I wonder if it is difficult for you to notice how you are feeling at work because you are so focused and have a bit of tunnel vision. If that's the case, it would be good for you to be able to check in with yourself just to be able to gauge when you are feelings stressed or irritated—recognize your angry state of mind. If you can, then I can show you things you can do to help yourself calm down. I also wonder if it also contributes to how your staff perceives you—that you sound annoyed even though you don't realize it. Again, tracking more closely how you are feeling will help with this.

The other part of anger, as I mentioned before, is not just about biting your tongue but also about using your feelings as information. For example, do you feel that your supervisor puts too much pressure on you; are your expectations and hers the same? Are there problems at work between you and your supervisor that you need to talk about with her and solve or between you and particular staff? Are there ways *your supervisor can be more supportive of you that would help you not push yourself so hard or help you when you notice staff struggling?*

The other part is again what I mentioned before. Growing up in a chaotic family where you weren't ever safe, you became wired to be hypervigilant and, through no fault of your own, learned to imitate the behaviors of those around you. Underneath what others see as irritation is, I suspect, anxiety, which is always there to some degree and gets worse under stress. That's another reason to be assertive and solve problems that are bothering you. You couldn't do this as a child, but you can now as an adult. This is part of rewiring your brain, upgrading the software, letting people know how you feel and what you need.

Part of helping with this rewiring is realizing that irritation is anxiety, telling yourself that these are reactions from the past, and you are now an adult and can handle them differently. The other part is trying to figure out what else you are feeling besides anger or anxiety—what are you worried about, afraid of, hurt by? The goal is to increase your range of emotions, so others can better understand how you feel and so you can use these feelings as information for solving problems.

Does this make sense?

Brett. *As I mentioned before, it makes sense to me that your sudden anger and attack against the cyclist are connected to the loss of your dad. You said that you really didn't have time to grieve and still haven't. I think that part of draining some of the irritability that your wife is noticing and helping prevent such incidents from coming up again in the future is tackling this grief more directly and I can help you do that.*

The other part of this is that I think you tend to be a guy who holds a lot of emotions in. I wonder if you sometimes aren't even aware of how you are feeling. Like the grief it becomes easy for feelings to build up until you eventually explode in some way. You learned to do this as a child because your family was like this, but it may not work so well for you now as an adult. I can imagine that your wife is wishing at times that you knew what you were thinking and feeling so she could feel more connected to you—do you think that is true?

So I'd like to help you learn to pay attention to your emotions more, to be able to identify them, share them with others, and use them as information about how you are and what you need. If you think it would be helpful, have your wife come here with you and we can talk about this. Maybe it will be a safe place for you to talk some things out or talk about ways she could help you with this.

Does this make sense?

What we are offering here is not a script per se but a way of demonstrating how the various elements of the treatment plan can be brought together. How you may present this will obviously depend on your personal style and approach. What is again essential is the tracking of agreement before moving on to our next step, the assignment of homework. We need to clear up any hesitations or questions; if we don't, the client's overall motivation and follow-through on homework is compromised.

ASSIGNING OF HOMEWORK

This is our last step in this first session. Let's summarize the assignments for each of our four clients.

Roger. Needs to track his emotional level several times a day to become more aware of his state of mind, looking for signs of irritation or anxiety; assign 1-day should-versus-want exercise to help him be more aware of what drives his actions and not just go on autopilot.

Sara. Like Roger, needs to track emotional state. When she begins to feel overwhelmed, she needs to ask herself what the particular problems are that she needs to address, any thoughts of concrete actions that she can take independently.

Marie. Like the others, tracking her state of mind. Of particular importance for her is not only noting irritation and using it as information to solve a particular problem but also asking herself what else she may be feeling—worried, sad, and so on—so she can begin to increase her emotional range.

Brett. There is a special assignment for Brett to help him deal directly with his unresolved grief. We are going to ask him to write three letters to his father. The basic instructions for such a letter are below (see Box 4.1).

This exercise can be used not only for unresolved grief—the death of a parent, the loss resulting from a miscarriage or abortion—but for any situation or relationship where there is a lack of closure, for example, a letter written to a former spouse following a divorce or to a supervisor following a job termination. Like empty-chair work where the client moves between two chairs,

---

BOX 4.1

Letter-Writing Exercise

You are going to write three letters. Preferably write these in longhand rather than on a computer. Do this in a quiet place at a time when you are not rushed or distracted. Write the letters in order. If you don't know where to start, start by writing that you don't know where to start and state how you are feeling right now. Write in a conversational or stream of consciousness style rather than formally plotting out what you want to say.

Letter 1
Say to the person whatever you would want to say to him or her if he or she were to come back and see you one more time. Try to get off your chest anything you wish you could say, both positive and negative. Try and make it as specific as possible; feel free to include memories, situations, events. Write until you feel you have no more to say.

Letter 2
Knowing his or her personality, write what you think the person would say if he or she actually received your letter.

Letter 3
If this person were to get your first letter, write the other's response, saying what you ideally would want to hear the other person say.

Bring all three letters into your next session.

role-playing both people and both sides of a dialogue, the letters push clients to voice both sides of the relationship, helping them to create a more balanced picture, as well as achieve some healing through the third letter. By handwriting the letters, the writer feels less of the performance pressure and permanence of the blank page of the computer, encouraging a stream of consciousness writing.

Depending on the nature of the relationship, the second letter can sometimes be skipped. If Brett had a good, open relationship with his father, for example, the second and third letters are likely to be identical. The second letter is important when the writer has a closed relationship, where his or her view of the other is narrow and one-dimensional. If Brett's father, for example, had been a no-nonsense, button-lipped military type of father, Brett's second letter may have reflected this side of his father's personality—"Dear Son, I received your letter. Thanks a lot. Hope you are well. Dad." The third letter allows Brett to hear what he needs to hear in order to heal.

Obviously doing such an assignment can be anxiety provoking and you shouldn't be surprised if clients find reasons to put it off for a few weeks—"I had to work overtime and didn't get a chance"; "There was a lot of commotion going on in the house all week and I couldn't find any quiet time." Clients do need to take time to do it and not rush through it to avoid their anxiety and simply get it out of the way. Be careful not to sound scolding but be persistent in reminding clients to complete the assignment. If you suspect that resistance is coming not from the anxiety of the emotional challenge but from an inability to see how it connects to the presenting problem, bring it up, making sure once again that you are on the same page.

SECOND SESSION

The second session for anger will focus on feedback on homework —ability to be aware of state of mind—and is a good time for teaching specific self-regulation skills: emotional freedom technique (EFT), meditation, deep breathing, and others. And as with anxiety, we want to offer clients a range of techniques so they have several to practice, to discover which works best for them, and, more important, to increase their sense of self-mastery through their knowing and feeling that they have several options that they can rely on.

If time permits, and if you are more psychodynamically oriented, you also may want to use part of the second session to explore a bit further into history. You may want to briefly talk with Marie, for example, more about her chaotic childhood. In the Boot Camp approach, however, the goal is not to begin unearthing her past trauma. Rather it is to reinforce for her once again both the notion that her anger is tied to learned childhood hypervigilance and that by recognizing her old triggers of the past and labeling them as being from the past, she can step back from them when they arise and shift her focus onto being an adult and onto the present.

And what if Brett is able to complete his letters and bring them in? He is likely to hand them to you to read. Hand them back and ask him to read them aloud, and get ready for the outpouring of grief. Your goal here is to simply be the compassionate listener. When he is done, you may want to circle back and gently ask questions about some of the content: "You mentioned the summer vacation when you were 8 years old—can you tell more about it?" or "You said that you wanted your father to be proud of you. How could he have best expressed this?"

The aim here is not to heap on more content but rather to stimulate more emotion by verbalizing details. You can also ask if there is anything that he found himself saying that surprised him, indicating that he had in fact moved to a deeper emotional level. Finally, at the end, say to Brett how much you appreciate his doing the assignment and taking such a huge emotional challenge, again underscoring your role as an ideal parenting figure.

If you are planning on bringing in family or friends to the third session, spend a few minutes preparing for this. Ask Sara or Roger, for example, if they would like to bring their spouses in next time and what they would like to talk about and get most out of the session. Sara may want to talk about Frank's control and how her resentment spills into the shopping she does. Roger may want to talk with Kelly about his feeling unappreciated or together how they can avoid arguments from turning into World War III. And while it is unlikely that Marie would invite her supervisor to a therapy session, she may need help in deciding whether to arrange a meeting with her supervisor and someone from human resources or her supervisor's supervisor or need help deciding what to make the primary focus or how to present her own concerns. The third session could then be used to map out an agenda with her for such a meeting or for her role-playing what she would like to say.

So you have some options. A priority needs to be placed on following up on homework and self-regulation skill training as a way of building on growing awareness and actively dealing with the presenting issues. The longer-range goals of increasing emotional flexibility, moving toward the adult, are exactly that—longer term and a matter of continued practice that you can encourage and monitor over time.

THIRD SESSION: FAMILY AND FRIENDS

Let's assume that Roger and Sara do bring their partners into the 3rd session. Let's talk about the goals and process for each.

Roger and Kelly. As mentioned in Chapter 3, our initial goal when family or friends come into a session is to help them feel welcomed and relaxed. We need to see them not as clients but as consultants, and our overall goal is to help accomplish by the end of the session what the client most wanted to cover. We are trying to help Roger, for example, be assertive and say to Kelly what he has a difficult time saying to her at home. We want to help them both have a deeper conversation than they normally have together, to uncover underlying softer emotions, to talk about intentions and motivations, and to define concrete behaviors that each can do to change dysfunctional patterns.

So we welcome Kelly, thank her for coming, ask if she and Roger have talked about the focus of the meeting. We ask her about herself to help build rapport and allow her to relax. We also may take the initiative and before moving into the session agenda ask her about her own perceptions about Roger's anger or their periodic explosive arguments. The aim here is to see how well her perceptions match those of Roger, to gather a more rounded picture of their interactions. She may say, for example, that she too is surprised by how quickly and suddenly small issues explode to the surface and the extent of Roger's anger, or no, she actually often feels she is walking on eggshells because she easily senses Roger's irritation. As we did with anxiety, we are looking for ways the partners can support each other. "Did you know," we might ask Roger, "that Kelly walks on eggshells at times? Can you tell? Is there something Kelly can do to help you when she senses your irritability? Kelly, is there something Roger can do when he seems irritable to help you not feel so cautious and worried?"

What we want are concrete behaviors: "Yes," says Roger, "it would be good if Kelly could just ask how I'm feeling." Show me, you say, how she needs to say that. "Yes," says Kelly, "it would be good if we could take a few minutes to just emotionally check in with each other for a few minutes when we both get home from work." Great, you say, tell me how you imagine best doing that.

Managing escalating arguments. In situations like Roger and Kelly's where arguments can quickly escalate, the couple needs to have ways to concretely stop the escalation. This is a matter of individual awareness—realizing that emotions are taking over—and having behavioral ways of self-regulating and being adult. A bit of education for the couple is helpful here. Here is what you might say:

When couples begin to get emotional and argue, the issue is no longer what they are talking about but the emotion in the room. Anger causes people to get tunnel vision, to be unable to process what the other is saying, to get fixated on getting the other to understand your point or getting the last word. The goal at that point is not to solve the problem but to put out the emotional fire in the room.

Anything you say at this point, no matter how benign it may seem, is likely, because of tunnel vision, to be misinterpreted—words are like gasoline thrown on a fire. So your first line of defense in putting out the fire is to be quiet and listen. Now this can often feel difficult because your initial reaction is that you are giving in and letting the other control the conversation. You need to actively say to yourself that you are not giving in but rather realizing that the other is struggling and helping him or her to calm down. If you don't feed the fire, but simply nod your head and listen, the other will initially ramp up—hurl an insult, say something provocative—to try and get you back in the fight because you are breaking the pattern. But if you don't take the bait, the other person will vent and then begin to calm down.

If this is too difficult to do, if both of you are too upset to simply listen, then one of you needs to be adult and move to your second line of defense and call a time-out. It would probably be helpful for us to map out a first aid plan right now for you both if the argument is getting out of control.

The goal of the first aid plan is to break the escalating pattern, allow time for cooling off rather than have further damage be inflicted, and let the other who felt cut off know that the conversation will in fact continue. A summary of the steps of the first aid plan is on the following page (see Box 4.2).

The couple needs to agree in the session on a nonverbal signal that either person can use to call a time-out at home. Why nonverbal? Because to simply announce in an angry tone, "I'm not talking about this anymore!" will only escalate the other's anger further. A large kitchen timer is best, as it is clearly visible. It is set and placed at home where the other person can see it. Because the pattern is broken and the other is likely to initially escalate further, it needs to be stressed that the one calling the time-out

---

BOX 4.2

First Aid Plan for Escalating/Violent Couples

- Stop talking and listen to help reduce the emotions and calm the other down
- If both are upset and have difficulty listening, call for a time-out to cool off:
  - Indicate time-out with agreed-on nonverbal signal.
  - Set timer for 45 minutes.
  - Do whatever you need to do not to reengage.
  - Return when timer goes off; if either one is still upset, reset timer.
  - If both are calm, try talking about the problem again; if it begins to escalate, stop.
  - Talk about the problem only when couple is completely calm.

---

absolutely needs to do what he or she needs to do not to reengage—lock him- or herself in the bathroom or car and drive away if necessary. After the timer goes off, the couple can try to talk calmly. If unable to, they reset the timer or wait until the next day. The goal here is to separate self-regulation from problem solving.

Finally, the steps in the first aid plan need to be written down and given to couples to put where they can easily refer to them at home—the refrigerator is ideal. Once tunnel vision sets in, it is difficult to remember the steps, so a quick reference is important.

Back to Roger. All this can be mapped out with Roger and Kelly as a way of dealing with Roger's presenting concern. But he also may want to talk in the session about feeling overresponsible, his desire for Kelly to appreciate him more, his desire to have her do more so he can do less. Again, the goals are to help him be assertive, for her to hear his concerns without feeling defensive, for the partner to voice her complementary needs, and for both of them to walk out with a concrete plan: Specifically how can Kelly show appreciation? Does she feel underappreciated at times herself? And what can Roger concretely do to acknowledge her? Can they come up with a concrete plan right now in the session for redistributing responsibilities so neither one feels overresponsible and resentful? Focus on process, take leadership, and help them move forward toward problem solving rather than getting stuck in the weeds of the past.

Sara and Frank. Our goals with Sara and Frank are similar to those of Roger and Kelly. We need to incorporate Frank into the session while focusing on Sara's primary goals for the session. It may be her talking with Frank about his seeming control; it may be helping him better understand her spending sprees; it may be his knowing what to do when she begins to feel overwhelmed besides stepping in and taking over. Like Roger, we want to help Sara be assertive—to express her emotions and desires clearly in an adult, rather than as a victim.

We need to be more attuned to the process with this couple than we probably needed to be with Roger. Because Sara is particularly sensitive to power and control, she needs to feel that we are clearly in her corner, advocating for her, and not unintentionally being perceived by her as aligning with Frank against her. Being aware of this at the start and even saying this aloud to her when planning the session can help avoid this pattern. We need to tightly track the process carefully in the room, watching that Sara doesn't get defensive or Frank doesn't begin to shut down or simply accommodate.

That said, as with Kelly, we not only need to help Frank not feel ganged up on, but also help him feel safe to present his side of the relationship, to help him realize that what Sara sees as control are his own softer underlying emotions. We want them both to walk out with a concrete plan, for Frank to know specifically what to do, when to help Sara when she feels overwhelmed, for example, by giving her a hug and calmly helping her partialize problems, or define concrete actions Sara can take when she feels Frank is being micromanaging or she is beginning to feel resentful, such as writing out how she feels and showing it to Frank or contacting her sister when the computer is calling her name. As with Roger and Kelly we want them both to feel that the enemy is not the other but the dysfunctional patterns. Our goal is to help them recognize the patterns and have ways of behaviorally changing them.

All this may take more than one couple session, and at some point you may wonder if the couple in fact needs couple therapy rather than just limited or periodic consultation sessions. If Roger and Kelly are not able to successful initiate the first aid plan, if Frank or Sara's resentments are more widespread, if Roger and Kelly differ in their approaches to key topics—parenting, sex, money, the power issues of couples—or if their communication skills are poor, then couple therapy may be necessary. As with other issues, you can uncover this by asking the hard questions and making the difficult statements—"You both seem to be struggling; I'm wondering if some separate couple therapy sessions might be helpful to you both"—and seeing what they both say next.

If both say yes, the clinical issue becomes one of deciding how to incorporate the individual work with that of the couple. Does Roger or Sara want to go ahead and start couples therapy with someone and come in periodically to check in around individual goals? Do they want to do both at the same time? Consider what in your own assessment would be the most productive focus. Even though the individual and couple goals interlock with each other, do you believe that the client can focus on both without getting scattered or overwhelmed? There is no right answer here. The issue needs to be decided by open conversation, raising concerns and options, and seeing where the motivation is the greatest.

FURTHER SESSIONS

Further sessions will focus on both the short- and longer-term goals. We will be checking in with Brett about his emotional state following his expression of grief; with Roger about his overresponsibility, his awareness of accommodation, his ability to be assertive, to focus on wants, and to take risks in trust; with Marie about her ability to self-regulate, to use anger as information, and to solve problems, her ability to increase her emotional flexibility and express softer emotions and to recognize when her hypervigilance is sensing a threat from her past and when she is acting in a more proactive, adult way. Homework assignments will concretely move between each of these goals, encouraging clients to take acceptable risks.

We will be looking for where clients get stuck, where difficulties arise, where skills and behaviors need to be fine-tuned. Rather than falling into a pattern in which clients need to be propped up by us each and every week, once the tasks are clear and implemented, spread sessions out so clients can increase their self-confidence by seeing their own gains and learning to turn to others for support. We want them to see us as a resource, to see our office as a safe place to measure success and sort out struggle; we want to help them be accountable and always want to encourage them to move forward without slipping into dependency.

ANGER AND MEDICATION

Just as medication can help break the cycle of anxiety, so too can it be helpful in breaking the cycle of anger. Medication can help slow the flaring up of anger so that someone like Marie is less reactive and has the space to put self-regulation techniques into place. It can help someone like Sara or Roger become less anxious when being assertive so they have a greater opportunity to build on their risks and success. Again, raise this in the initial session and suggest a consult as another aspect of the overall treatment plan.

Following the approach used in Chapter 3, here is a summary of the Boot Camp approach to anger:

Treatment Map For Anger

OVERALL TREATMENT GOALS AND TASKS
- Recognize angry state of mind
- Take control/self-regulate: tools and techniques (breathing, EFT, meditation, journaling, etc.)
- Increase emotional flexibility

- Use anger as information; determine if there is a problem to fix, needs to be addressed
- Link to personality: hypervigilance; persecutor role; resentment from being in rescuer/victim roles; move toward adult

SESSION 1 • GOALS AND TASKS

- Assess: Awareness of state of mind; hypervigilance; overre-sponsibility/resentment; unresolved grief; self-regulation; medication; personal/family history
- Change emotional climate (focus on soft emotions, education, leadership, listen and support)
- Link problem to personality (show relationship triangle, show how rescuer/victim roles move to persecutor roles; define *adult*)
- Educate: Angry state of mind; self-regulation tools; anger as information; anger as underlying anxiety; moving out of rescuer/victim roles; resolve grief; increase emotional range
- Present treatment plan: Self-regulation; anger as information; resolving underlying anxiety; being adult
- Get on same page (track process like bloodhound)—making sure clients understand link between plan and anger
- Assign homework: Check-ins regarding emotional state, triggers, underlying emotions; letter-writing for grief

SESSION 2 • GOALS AND TASKS

- Feedback on homework
- Teach self-regulation: EFT, meditation, other techniques
- Plan agenda for family/friend session if applicable
- Homework: Practice techniques; use anger as information

SESSION 3 • GOALS AND TASKS

- Feedback on homework
- Family/friends: Discuss how other can help with

self-regulation; solve concrete problems that lead to perse-cutor response

- Fine-tune treatment plan: Determine where stuck—as-signments too big; need to develop skills; need medica-tion to break cycle; something else?—explore

FURTHER SESSIONS

- Assign homework
- Focus on self-regulation; ability to define other emotions; ability to use anger as information; ability to be assertive
- Accountability—use sessions to help clients stay on track
- Determine what additional supports are needed for success

This concludes our discussion of anger. In Chapter 5, we will look at the final disorder explored in this book, as I describe the Boot Camp approach to depression.

CHAPTER FIVE

Treatment Map for Depression

HAROLD IS 53 YEARS OLD and has been married for 30 years. His wife suffered a brain aneurysm 2 years ago and she quickly went from being a responsible bank manager and energetic woman to someone who is unable to drive and is forgetful, moody, and emotionally dependent on Harold. Harold used to own a car repair business but sold it because of the long hours and lack of health insurance and now works in security. He appears worn out, admits to drinking more than he used to, and is angry at . . . what happened. He came in because his doctor referred him and says that even talking about his situation is hard: "I've always been the kind of guy who tends to keep things inside."

The divorce was Abby's idea. After 10 years of marriage she was done—tired of the petty arguments, her husband's criticism, the lack of affection. While at first she felt relieved and even energized being on her own, now she was beginning to crash—sleeping more, feeling lethargic, ruminating, dreading weekends. She has friends, she likes her work, but on a bad day she isn't sure what she has to look forward to.

Karen seems exhausted even as she talks. She rattles off a list of physical ailments: irritable bowel syndrome, migraines, and back pain, and while she has never been officially diagnosed with it, she believes she has fibromyalgia. She has always been a homemaker. Her children are now leaving home—one is already in college and another is about to start—and she complains that her husband is a loner who would rather hunt and fish than spend time with her; she says, "We've been living parallel lives for years." She has no real friends, mostly just acquaintances from church, and says that members of her extended family never think of anyone but themselves. When asked what she likes to do, she says, "Unfortunately, there's not much that I'm good at."

Like anxiety and anger, depression can have different faces. But in contrast to that of the other two, the landscape of depression can quickly get murky, especially when we look at the statistics. While the incidence of major depressive disorder is cited at 6.7% of the population, bipolar disorder at 2.6%, and dysthymic disorder at 1.5% (Kessler, Chiu, Demler, & Walters, 2005), the percentage of people in the United States reporting depression, according to a World Health Organization study, stands at 19.2%, second in the world behind France, at 21% (Renick, 2011). Researchers such as Andrews and Thompson (2009) make a similar case that while other mental health disorders are around the 5% range, depression is 4–5 times higher, indicating the situational nature of most depression.

Why the difference? Some, like Andrew Weil (2011), attribute the high depression rate to the fact that our brains are not equipped to deal with 21st-century life, with its technology of distraction and overload. Ronald Kessler, a professor of health care policy at Harvard Medical School, points out that while there is no change in biological depression, "what's going up is mild depression. . . . We have an expectation that everything's going to turn out perfect but it doesn't" (quoted in Renick, 2011).

Psychiatrists interested in evolutionary explanations, such as Anderson Andrews and Paul Thompson (2009), actually view depression not as symptom of expectations and culture but as the body's way of processing real-world problems. Rumination, a symptom of depression, is in their view attributable to the way our brains have evolved to help us stay focused and unravel quandaries. Their research suggests that those who are slightly depressed actually make better, more reality-based decisions than those who are not. As such they hesitate to immediately medicate but instead see treatment as helping the client work through the problems that they are mentally circling around, which in turn relieves the depression.

When we look at Harold, Abby, and Karen, we can see in their presentations this depressive mix of stress and situation. Harold is dealing not only with loss related to his changed wife, his business, and the circumstances of his life but also ongoing stress, the male tendency to show anger and an agitated form of depression, and learned internalization. Abby's grief seems less complex, caused by the loss of a relationship, regardless of whether she initiated it or not, and the sometimes overwhelming challenge of starting a new chapter in her life. And then there is Karen, who in her presentation seems to have many of the signs of dysthymia—that long-term undertow of the depression, the constant graying of the world, the depressive lifestyle no doubt made worse by her children leaving home and her empty marriage that leaves her feeling miserable and stuck.

The Boot Camp Approach to Depression

If anxiety is about the runaway horse, depression, from the Boot Camp perspective, is about feeling stuck or trapped. What we are not talking about here are the roughly 2–7% of people with major depression or with bipolar illness or those with complex and severe PTSD, in which depression is a major ingredient of their distress; these individuals are not appropriate for the brief Boot Camp model because of the nature of their illness and the higher level of risk. What we are talking about is the rest, the 12–17% with mild to moderate situational depression. Here the Boot Camp approach can be both effective and efficient because of its focus on helping clients untangle problems and move forward behaviorally.

When clients like Harold say that they feel as though they are standing at the bottom of a well looking up, able to see the sky but feeling that there is no way out, we can say that our job is to help him find a way. When Abby's lack of energy or loneliness or uncertainty about the future leaves her feeling overwhelmed, we want to find acceptable risks that she can take to break the patterns. And though Karen seems plagued by physical ailments, they are no doubt aggravated by her mindset. She complains but does little behaviorally to change—because she is afraid, perhaps, or because she doesn't know how, or because her depressed voice says, "Why bother?"—and as a result she is depressed because in large part her life itself is depressing.

Depression, the relationship triangle, and the core dynamic. Just as we were able to place anxiety and anger within the framework of the relationship triangle, we can do this with depression. If we look at the rescuer role, we can imagine how those with such a personality would be susceptible to depression—the burdens of overresponsibility, caretaking, doing the right thing, perfectionism, the self-criticism—the weight of it all and the disconnection from one's own self accumulating over time. But there is also victimization; this is what we hear in the stories of Harold, Abby, and Karen, where each is reactive and overwhelmed by problems seeming to fall down on them, fueling their sense of powerlessness and feeling stuck. Finally, we have the potential for acting out—Brett's grief and his assault on the cyclist come to mind, as does Harold's escalation to binge drinking; we could imagine Karen lashing out explosively if she feels frustrated by her husband or her family's neglect for too long.

Which brings us back to the adult and the core dynamic. In assessing Harold and Karen, and even Abby, with her more straightforward grief, we are looking for a gap, however small, between what the client does and doesn't do under such stress and life changes and what an adult would do. Even though clients may be struggling with real-life problems, we are still looking to see how childhood coping strategies no longer are working and how the circumstances and relationships are only reigniting old wounds. If being stuck is the solution, what is the problem?

What keeps Harold, for example, from reaching out to others for support, both with his emotions and with caring for his wife? Does he have that rescuer belief that he can't trust others and has to do things on his own? Is his anger an indication that his emotional range is limited, making it difficult for him to feel his sadness and openly grieve? Is Karen's isolation, like Harold's, a sign of distrust, her resigned acceptance of her husband's detachment and the lack of intimacy between them part of a larger difficulty she has with being assertive? Is it the result of a lack of skill or a fear of taking a risk?

And even though Abby finally took active steps to break away from her critical and unaffectionate husband, we are curious about how this fits into the larger context of her history and her life. Had she had other relationships in which there was criticism and lack of affection in the past? How did she learn to accept such treatment? Is leaving a sign of her taking a level of risk and a clear breaking of patterns or more of her reaching the same bottom line as before and essentially continuing her history? What does she need to understand and do differently if she is to avoid falling into a similar relationship again in the future?

Finally, it's tempting to respond to the question of why these clients get stuck by seeing the depression as largely the culprit: If Harold wasn't depressed he wouldn't be drinking so much or feel resentful, Abby would be moving on more easily, Karen would be out making friends or having a heart-to-heart with her husband rather than internalizing. Yes and no. Again, since we are dealing with primarily situational depression, the process quickly becomes circular. Depression certainly undercuts the ability to cope and solve the problems, but, we wonder, to what degree does the client's inability to cope and solve the problems fuel the depression? In the action-oriented focus of the Boot Camp approach, this is an important part of the puzzle that we and the client need to explore.

TREATMENT GOALS FOR DEPRESSION

As with anxiety and depression, there are overlapping and specific goals that we need to address:

Recognize the depressed state of mind. As with the thinking patterns of anxiety and anger, the depressive mind has its own voice, with which we are all familiar; it says, "Why bother? It will never change. I deserve this. This is my fault. Life always turns out this way." So too does rumination, which, as mentioned earlier, is one of the symptoms of depression—Abby, for example, replaying over and over scenes from her marriage, as well as the future-oriented, worst-case scenarios that come with accompanying anxiety; Harold lying in bed at night worrying about whether his wife will get worse or if they have enough money to cover the medical bills.

Generally the depressive mind fades in and out over the course of the day, even if subtly. The goal is to have clients recognize when they are getting lost in those thoughts—Abby thinking about the marriage rather than focusing at work, or Karen telling herself that nothing will ever change when her husband goes off hunting. Again, clients don't need to deconstruct these thoughts, as they would do in traditional cognitive-behavior therapy or dialectical behavioral therapy, but label their state of mind—"My depressed mind is ramping up!"—and then take action to override it.

Calm the depressed mind: tools and techniques. Just as we developed a repertoire of first aid tools and techniques to stop the runaway horse of anxiety and to put out the fire of anger, we need to provide such a repertoire to clients with depression. Not surprisingly our cache is pretty much the same: regular journaling and writing down thoughts; becoming mindful, focusing on the sights and sounds right there in the external world; engaging in distracting and flow-type activities that are able to pull the client out of the negative state of mind, such as listening to a favorite piece of music, reading a good novel, watching a movie, practicing an engaging hobby (such as woodworking or painting); exercising; using EFT; practicing meditation; engaging in social interaction, as in calling up a friend, not to necessarily talk about oneself, but to focus on someone else and talk about his or her life; having lunch with a colleague; joining a bowling team. A list can be compiled, and techniques can be taught within the first two sessions.

Just a note on writing: Writing can be particularly helpful for depression, not only for discharging thoughts on the page but also for countering the negative state of mind. A particularly useful exercise is the one mentioned for anxiety: having clients write down all the positive things that occurred over the course of day, taking 5–10 minutes to do so. Again, focusing on small details is important—the person who opened the door at the bank, the fact that the weather was nice, that the neighbor said hello and asked how you were. These help train the mind to notice the positives and gradually help insulate it from depressive thinking.

Recognize and act on strong emotions. Clients with depression often talk about feeling numb, as though there were a blanket over their emotions, or they had a constant dull ache. Strong emotions are important as indicators of needs and problems and Boot Camp clients are encouraged to look, label, and act on them. For example, when Harold productively channels his anger—talking to his wife's doctor to understand better what happened and why, or talking to his minister to help him make sense of this change in his life—he stops the resentment from simply smoldering and adding to his distress. Similarly, if Karen finds herself with the unexpected urge, however brief and subtle, to call up a church acquaintance, or Abby is motivated to take off on a Friday and go see her sister two states away, they are both not only breaking out of their depressive behavioral patterns but also developing trust in gut reactions that can be an ongoing source of motivation and direction.

Take action: Feel better by doing. Taking action is the key to our approach to depression. The antidote to feeling stuck and trapped is to do something. It is not about doing the "right" thing that rescuers can obsess about, but about the movement, the doing in itself that can break the hold that depression seems to have.

We're back to Morita and his notion of focusing on what you need to do next rather than getting caught in the quagmire of emotions. This is particularly applicable and important for depression precisely because the depressed mind creates the opposite notion: that I need to feel better in order to act. So Abby and Karen sit at home and are miserable because they don't feel like going out; they often seek therapy, wanting the therapist to somehow unlock the nut of the emotion so they can then begin to act. As with Morita, the Boot Camp approach says to do it even if you don't feel like it, and your feelings will begin to catch up. Just as we urge anxious clients to not let the runaway horse of anxiety control their lives, we urge depressed clients to not let the undertow of depression control theirs.

As with the other disorders, the clinical challenge is to determine an acceptable behavioral risk that the client is willing to take and what supports are needed for success. If a client is depressed because he was laid off from his job and spends the day sitting on the couch drinking beer and watching *CSI* marathons, he is going to stay depressed as long as he sits on the couch. He needs to somehow get himself down to the employment office even if he doesn't feel like it. Is he willing to do this? Does his wife need to get him up early, make him breakfast, and drive him down there? Does a friend or even the therapist need to come back at 9:00 on Tuesday morning and pick him up and stay with him so he doesn't back out once he is there?

Similarly, if Karen is willing to attend a midweek church potluck supper, does one of her church acquaintances need to give her a ride and maybe sit next to her at the table? Does Harold need help in his therapy session figuring out what he wants to ask his wife's physician? Is Abby willing to act on her seemingly out-of-the-blue idea of going back to school by making an appointment to talk to the counselor at the community college? What help does she need to make it happen? Here is where assigning homework is often enough to motivate clients; Abby's knowing that she is going to have to report back to the therapist next week will push her into action.

And what if clients say they can't? Again, resistance is a solution, not the problem. Sometimes the "I can't" statements are a signal that you and a client are not on the same page. They are not able to see the connection between their view of the problem or expectations of therapy and what you are proposing—for example, your urging Harold to reach out for support seems irrelevant to him, since in his mind the medical bills worry him the most or Karen was expecting a therapist who would empathize with her ailments, rather than encourage her to take action. Track the process, check for agreement, stop if there is resistance, educate and clarify. If you hear ambivalence, ask if clients are willing to just give it a try, to see if your approach makes a difference.

Most often, however, the source of the resistance is anxiety; that is, what you are asking them to do is too big a step for them. If they are easily overwhelmed—prone to having a victim personality—even a relatively small step can seem insurmountable. Or if they have the personality of a rescuer, they can easily become anxious from the pressure to both please you and do it right. Negotiate an acceptable risk that they feel they can manage, track carefully and ensure agreement, and then determine with them what supports are needed for their success.

Resistance can also come from transference. Because of the critical voice and low self-esteem that come with a depressed state of mind, it's easy for clients to hear this criticism echoed in your own presentation. Couple this with their own childhood wounds, and it's easy to stir up resistance. Given Abby's history with her critical husband, for example, and her current state of mind, we can imagine that what we intend as a simple request can sound to Abby like a demand or that she will take as a scolding our disappointment when she fails to do her homework.

We're back to determining quickly what we need to do to avoid replicating the problem in the therapeutic relationship. For clients with depression we need to be sensitive to their own critical voices and be both gentle and positive but also acutely aware of misinterpretation. When we sense, for example, that Abby, in her defensiveness or apologetic response, is likely feeling scolded, we need to stop once again and clarify: "I'm concerned that you may be feeling right now that I'm annoyed with you. I'm sorry if I seem to sound that way, but I'm not annoyed. I'm just wondering why you weren't able to do the homework assignment, if maybe it felt too difficult or if my instructions were too unclear." Then see what she says next. What we are looking for is not the content of the answer to our question—why she didn't do the homework—but the process, that her resistance is down, she feels safe, and she is back in step with us.

Finally, what seems like resistance may be the powerful undertow of depression itself. The exhaustion, obsessing, or negative thinking is so overpowering that clients can't fully engage in treatment. This is when medication may be useful, to help break the cycle and jump-start some action. Bring this up with clients to gauge their perspective. For those reluctant to take medication, ask why. Sometimes it is fear of side effects or of having to stay on them forever; for others, taking medication is a sign of weakness.

Counter these arguments with information. Assure clients that they can discuss with their doctor their concern about side effects, that the medication need not be ongoing but can be helpful in the short term to break a downward spiral, that their depression and life situation has a real physiological impact on their body and brain, and that, like other medications, antidepressants can be helpful for restoring the brain to normal levels. Finally, they are not trapped. If they try the medication and don't find it helpful, they can gradually stop.

Facilitate the grief process. Depression that clients present is often emotionally multifaceted—trapped feelings combined with anxiety about the future, suppressed anger combined with self-criticism, grief combined with self-criticism and worry about the future. Each of our three clients is dealing with some level of loss and grief: Harold has the loss of the wife he used to have as well as the loss of his business and change in his lifestyle, Karen feels a sense of loss as her children move on and one chapter in her life ends, and Abby is dealing with the loss of a relationship and all that this entails. And with one loss often comes the stirrings of others. Harold, like Brett earlier, may not have fully grieved the loss of a parent, or Karen, so preoccupied and hampered by physical problems, may grieve the healthy young woman that she once was.

So we look for grief and label it, and the labeling—"You are dealing with a real and normal sense of loss and grief"—can describe for clients the landscape of grief so they know how the process naturally proceeds. We can assign the letter-writing exercise to facilitate the process. We encourage clients to allow themselves to feel what they are feeling but also behaviorally continue to move forward, rather than letting their emotions drive them.

Risk reduction: focusing on the core dynamic. Reducing risk and centering on the core dynamic become our long-term goals, which we map out for clients in the first session. As we did for anxiety and anger, we are looking to upgrade childhood coping styles by encouraging clients to go against their grain and approach problems in a more adult way. Here is a quick list of longer-term treatment goals:

- *Develop assertiveness.* Assertiveness is the adult antidote to good-kid rescue behaviors, victim anxiety and helplessness, and persecutor anger and aggression.
- *Approach anxiety.* Practice extending one's comfort zone by taking acceptable risks in order to become more flexible and increase self-esteem.
- *Push back against shoulds and the critical voice; focus on wants.* The first step is helping clients recognize shoulds and self-scolding. The next step is acting in spite of

obstacles. The final step is substituting wants for shoulds to break out of rescue behavior.

- *Take concrete action to solve problems rather than obsessing over doing it "right" or giving up.* This is action as antidote to perfectionism and victim underresponsibility.
- *Increase emotional flexibility and use anger as information about needs.* Depression, like anxiety and anger, can be a cover for other feelings. Clients need to cultivate an emotional range. Freud's definition of depression as anger turned inward is particularly apt. Clients need to use anger as information about what they need and where there are problems to solve.
- *Develop a self-care lifestyle.* Those prone to depression need to reduce their risk by developing a healthier lifestyle— regular sleep, healthy diet, exercise and self-centering practices (yoga, journaling, meditation) to reduce stress.
- *Develop a diversity of social supports.* More than anxiety and anger, depression thrives on isolation. Those prone to depression need to have social supports and need to be encouraged to develop and interact with them even when they don't feel like it. Finally, risk is reduced by not putting all the eggs in one basket. Having multiple sources of support is better than having just one or two.

While all these points apply to people with depression, we would obviously initially focus on the points that are most appropriate for any given client. We may encourage Harold to use his anger as information, while at the same time explore with him other emotions that may lie beneath. The focus with Karen may be on her taking social risks so she is less isolated, as well as being assertive and proactively addressing the problems with her husband. Abby may need help developing a self-care lifestyle of exercise and meditation or, given her new status, begin to expand her social group rather than relying on her good married friends. We focus most on the holes—what is lacking in the client's world—but don't need to get bogged down in developing precise recipes. What we are encouraging most at the start is breaking out—change for change's sake, stopping dysfunctional patterns—in order to counter the criticism and trapped feelings of depression.

COUNTERTRANSFERENCE AND DEPRESSION

Discussion of encouraging and not replicating the problem brings us to the topic of countertransference issues that are likely to surface when treating depression. One is that it is easy to work harder than the clients. This can come from a couple of sources. One is that in our empathy for their suffering, we essentially move too quickly. As we are not in their situation, it is easy for us to see the path through the woods that for them is immersed in fog, and we instinctively try to push them along as they drag their feet. While we are seeking change for change's sake, we also need to slow down and make sure they are able to stay in lockstep with us.

Similarly, we can work harder as a way of trying to counter the frustration we may feel when facing the inertia and critical voice of the depressed mind. We want to be positive, be hopeful, and encourage action, but again we don't want to simply push clients along. We want successful behaviors and acceptable risks. Rather than pushing harder, we need to talk about the critical voice and inertia directly—label them, normalize them, help clients become aware of them—and then encourage clients to move against these negative factors.

Which brings us to the other major countertransference danger: Instead of working too hard, we don't work hard enough. Depression is contagious, and if we ourselves are in a depressed state of mind we too can begin to feel like the client—a sense of "Why bother?" and of giving up, being burned out, or having a feeling of being overwhelmed and inert ourselves. Our first line of defense is to recognize when this is taking hold—when our own energy and interaction in the session wanes, when pessimism creeps in and homework assignments are skipped or not followed up on. We need to treat ourselves the way we need to treat the client, recognizing and behaviorally countering these feelings. Finally, we need to seek support. Talking to a colleague or supervisor not only can help us put our reactions in perspective, but also can build in some accountability that can help us stay on track.

Finally, as mentioned earlier, we are susceptible to replicating the clients' dysfunctional relationship patterns, inadvertently finding ourselves, for example, feeling critical of Abby or pulling away from Karen the way their husbands do. Our antidote is once again awareness, listening for and defining as quickly as possible for ourselves the relationship patterns we most need to avoid.

Treatment Map for Depression: Content and Process

As we did with anxiety and anger, let's break down the crucial elements of the beginning sessions:

FIRST SESSION

While the energy and emotional tone in the room when meeting a new client suffering with depression can clearly be different than that of anxiety and anger, the terrain is similar. Once again we'll break the important first session down into segments:

Opening. The initial contact is the same as that of the other disorders—hearing a brief description of the problem, providing a brief introduction to the Boot Camp approach—and the opening is similar as well. We want to let clients tell their story, Harold about his wife's aneurysm, Karen about her physical problems and her family, Abby about her separation and pending divorce. As with anxiety and anger, we are looking for replication of symptoms in the session process—signs of the depressed state of mind with statements of hopelessness, helplessness, or self-criticism; low energy; difficulty staying focused; and obsessive thinking about the past and tunnel vision about the future—as a way of beginning our initial assessment.

We are also looking for the ability of clients to step outside of their comfort zones. For someone like Harold, who openly says that he is not one to talk about his thoughts and feelings, we want to see just how well he can, even at the beginning of the session, with gentle encouragement and prompting. Similarly, with someone like Karen, who all too readily can go on and on about her ailments, we want to inquire about resentment toward her husband or about her children leaving home and see if she can follow our lead. We are once again moving the client toward what is not in the room—the emotional and content holes.

Assessment. Here is a list of typical assessment questions. We will use the same format that we used for the anxiety and anger assessments.

Symptoms and Situation
How long have you been depressed? Has it become worse? How? (Differentiating between dysthymia and situational depression)

How does it affect your everyday functioning, for example, no energy, difficulty focusing, crying, irritability, isolation, physical ailments? How are your sleeping and eating patterns? (Vegetative symptoms and level of incapacitation)

Do you notice if it is better on some days than on others? What do you think makes it better? (Depression often goes up and down; trying to define beneficial factors)

Why are you seeking help now? Have you ever been in therapy before? If so, what was helpful or not helpful about it? (Self-motivated for treatment vs. pressured by others; check on past experience in order to know what to do and not do now)

What do you find yourself thinking about most? Is there one real-life problem, other than your depression, that you feel you need to address and solve? If so, what have you done to try to solve it? (Awareness of situational sources of depression; ability to take concrete action)

If you find yourself obsessing about one particular thing, can you ever "catch it" and make yourself think of something else? Do you have some way to stop it or not pay attention to it? (Ability to override the depressed mind)

Have you ever thought of suicide? Have you ever made any attempts? (Assessing suicidal risk; previous attempts increase risk)

Are you taking any medication for your depression? If so, do you feel that it helps? Have you talked to your doctor about your overall physical condition? (Medication effects, client compliance; need to rule out physical causes for symptoms, for example, unhealthy hormone or thyroid levels)

Do you use alcohol, marijuana, food, or anything else as a way to feel better? (Self-medicating)

When you try to make sense of why you are feeling the way you do now, what do you come up with? (Theory of problem)

Core Dynamics
Overall how do you cope with stress? How sensitive are you to others? How perfectionistic, self-critical? Do you ever bite your tongue to avoid conflict? Do others see you as someone who helps a lot of people and takes on a lot of responsibility? (Symptoms of rescuer behaviors)

Do you ever feel unappreciated or resentful that others are not carrying their own weight? What do you do when you feel this way? (Rescuers moving to the persecutor role)

Do you easily feel overwhelmed at times, feeling that there are too many problems coming at you at one time? If so, how do you handle these situations? (Symptoms of victim role)

What do you do when you get angry? Would others say that you are controlling or aggressive? (Symptoms of persecutor behaviors)

Can you easily feel a range of emotions—notice when you are sad or worried or frightened or angry? Is there one emotion that is easier for you to feel than others? (Emotional flexibility)

Is there a family history of depression, anxiety, or similar problems? Is there any history of psychiatric illness? (Genetic components of illness)

Is there any childhood history of emotional, physical, or sexual abuse? If yes, do you feel it continues to affect you now? How? (Impact of childhood wounds, coping style and its limits)

Self-Care

Do you have particular ways of dealing with stress? Do you exercise? Do you do any self-centering activities such meditation, journaling? (Stress-reduction tools)

Do you have friends? If you are having a hard time, is there someone you talk to? Are there social activities that you engage in? If you push yourself to go out somewhere do you feel better once you are there? (Social supports, ability to reach out)

This covers the basic framework of assessment according to the Boot Camp approach. Depending on your own models and your clinical style, you may focus on certain questions more than others or substitute others. What is again important is not getting bogged down in lengthy assessments; the assessment process will be continuing and refined as clients begin their homework and implement behaviors.

Changing the emotional climate. In order to change the emotional climate, we will use the same techniques that we did with anxiety and anger: looking for the holes in both content and unspoken emotions. Going where the client is not, we might ask Harold about feeling sad or lonely, since he can easily talk about his anger, or ask Karen what she is proud of or thankful for, since her words center so much on the negative.

We're also going to look for nonverbal signs of emotion, for example, picking up on it if we notice a deep sigh from Harold or that he is tearing up—"Harold, let me interrupt you for a minute. What just happened? You're looking sad right now"—and see if that helps him drop his defenses. We can also ask hard questions—asking Abby if she ever worries that she won't ever find another mate or if she ever regrets not leaving earlier, or asking Karen if she worries that her marriage will never change and she will remain lonely.

We can tell stories—composites of past clients who have moved through divorce or successfully met the challenge of dealing with catastrophic illness in the family, or if comfortable, describing a challenge from our own experience. While many find such stories inspiring, we need to be careful that clients don't mishear what we are saying as minimizing their pain or that making changes, which seem so overwhelming to them now, sound too easy to accomplish. If we sense such a negative response, we need to simply stop and clarify: "I don't want to give you the impression that this was easy for this person to do. I'm trying to give you a sense of hope, that others have struggled, just as you are, and have been able to move forward and find a sense of peace."

Finally, we can stir emotions by using the ideal voice, for example, verbalizing what Karen's husband might say in an ideal conversation about his preoccupations and withdrawal from her, or what Abby's husband ideally might say if he were to look back and realize how his criticism of Abby caused her to feel unloved. These can be powerful ways of cutting through the numbness of depression and setting the stage for behavioral change. If Karen or Abby said, for example, that they wished they could have such deep conversations with their husbands, the next step may be figuring out with them where they could start.

Education. Clients benefit not only from labeling grief but also from understanding the larger terrain of depression. We can state aloud to Abby that even though she initiated the separation, it makes absolute sense that now she is emotionally starting to crash; she has suffered a loss from which she needs to heal. Understanding this can help her not mistake her natural emotions for poor decisions. Mapping the terrain in time—letting her know that it often takes those going through divorce a year to feel that they have their feet solidly on the ground—helps her set realistic expectations for her own progress.

Similarly, we can explain to Harold that he is like a lot of other men who have learned to be strong and silent and that stress and depression often come out as anger and affect the serotonin levels in his brain that help counter his self-criticism. Showing him the relationship triangle can help him see how he has now been forced to adopt a caretaking rescuer role, and given its dynamics, his periodic bursts of anger make sense. It also shows him how the imbalance in his relationship and his feeling trapped in his situation fuel his depression. By creating outside supports and exploring ways to develop a sense of self apart from his caretaking responsibilities, he can gain a greater sense of control in his life, and this in turn may motivate him to take action.

And Karen, who feels plagued by illness and is lonely, angry, and resigned to the neglect of her husband and her extended family, needs to understand how her wishing and waiting for them to treat her better only perpetuates her sense of helplessness and state of depression. We show her the relationship triangle and the role of the adult to help her move out of her victim role. We empathize with her physical struggle and the way her condition can make her everyday world seem small, but we say that we assume that she has come into therapy because she wants to change this and that we want to help her build a better life in spite of the challenges she faces.

We're back to our physician analogy. Just as we feel less anxious and more hopeful once a physician describes for us the cause and course of our condition and gives us treatment options and time frames for improvement, so can clients who are dealing with normal grief and loss or the depression that comes from feeling trapped by life situations and problems feel better. Having a new and larger perspective ends the tunnel vision that comes with a depressed state of mind. Clients can begin to realize, if not yet feel, that though the depression causes them to feel powerless, there is in fact much that they can do.

PRESENTING THE TREATMENT PLAN

What does each of our clients need to feel better? What core dynamic keeps them from being more adult? Our overall approach for all is the same—the need to recognize the depressed state of mind and take active behavioral steps to counter it. Let's break it down for each of them. These are things we might say:

Harold. Over the past 2 years, Harold, you have gone through so many changes—dealing with not only your wife's brain aneurysm and her limitations but also the loss of your business that you enjoyed and the fact that you have dedicated yourself to your wife's care. As I mentioned before, it makes sense to me that you are angry and depressed. You're grieving and sad, though you try not to show it.

I think there are a couple of things we need to work on. One is that I'm worried that you are going to burn yourself out being the sole caretaker of your wife. I wonder if it would be useful to talk with the doctor about some home care for your wife just to give you a break, or to ask your son if he can help sometimes. I know you are reluctant to do that, *but again it's hard to shoulder this all on your own. I think if you had some time to yourself to get out with friends or do some of the things you enjoyed before, you would feel better.*

Since you are concerned about your anger, I think we also need to help you be more emotionally flexible. Underneath anger is often a lot of other feelings, and even today you looked sad at times. That's important to let yourself feel, even though it seems a bit unnatural for you. This is something we can work on together.

Does this make sense to you?

Abby. *You're going through a major life event and courageously took steps to change your life for the better. As I mentioned, it completely makes sense to me that the initial relief is beginning to wear off and you are feeling more depressed. This is the landscape of grief and loss that naturally comes with such a major change.*

On bad days when you feel lonely or worry about your future, this is your depression talking. It takes most folks several months to begin to feel better, and you are doing a good job of continuing to move forward with friends, and on your job, in spite of how you feel at times. You don't want to overwhelm yourself by pushing too hard, but you don't want to stand still either. Proactively mapping out plans in advance for weekends would probably help you dread them less.

While you are in this state of transition and open to new ideas, this also might be a good time to reflect on your marriage. Oftentimes when we decide to end a relationship we naturally come up with a picture of our relationship that is a bit too simple; for example, we decide that the marriage ended because our spouse was having an affair or was too critical. While such things may be true, these facts don't help us understand the nuances of the relationship, the other's perspective, or our contribution to the relationship dynamics. Having a clearer sense of this can help you better understand the lessons that the relationship can teach you so you can use them in future relationships.

So it might be useful for us to talk about this a bit or, if he is willing, to even have your husband come in for one or two sessions to simply explain things from his perspective, obviously not to stir old wounds, but to help you both have some closure and understanding.

Does this make sense to you?

This last suggestion about essentially creating an opportunity to deconstruct the marital relationship is invaluable in separation and divorce situations. As part of the decision-making and grief process each partner has to formulate an explanation for why things turned out the way they did, but the explanation, especially in the early stages, is often too simple and black and white—I left because he did this, because she treated me like that, because I should have done this. The simple explanation only leaves them with lessons too simple for future relationships—I need to avoid men who do that or I need to never do what I did before. Relationships are more nuanced and reflect the patterns created by both parties. Egregious behaviors are symptoms of and solutions to underlying emotions and problems. The moral of the story of a relationship becomes more honest and helpful when the individuals develop a more complex and balanced picture.

To encourage such reflection does not mean we need to shift to long-term therapy. In the Boot Camp approach, this can be explored in a few sessions. We don't need to walk through the relationship step by step; we can instead focus on the hard questions and use the letter-writing exercise to stimulate a broader perspective. We can invite the partner in to provide them both with a safe environment to have a deeper conversation, or we can encourage clients to have a conversation in person or via letters or emails on their own with the other to help them gain a more rounded picture and facilitate closure.

Karen. *You seem to be struggling with several things all at one time. We have your ongoing physical issues, and I can understand that not only do they leave you with pain and exhaustion but also emotionally can leave you feeling depleted. You have spent many years being a good mom for your children and now they are moving on, ending a chapter of your life. And where some couples now turn toward each other to start a new challenge and chapter, you and your husband are essentially living parallel lives.*

I think your depression comes partly from a sense of loss and partly from feeling that you're stuck and nothing will change. You're also iso-lated and lonely, and though you don't like feeling this way, it seems that it is difficult for you to reach out to others—to your husband to help him understand how you feel and what you would like changed, to your family who you feel doesn't care about you, to others who might become a friend or support. Instead you tend to withdraw and believe perhaps that others won't care. This is your depressed mind talking, but I suspect it is also something you learned long ago as child.

You came here looking to feel better and that is an important first step. While you can't change your husband or family, I think there are things you can do to help yourself feel better. It might be a good idea to invite your husband in, or even members of your family, so we can help them understand how you feel. Or we can map out what I call acceptable risks that you can take to help you feel less lonely, more productive, and less depressed. You seem to have high standards for yourself and easily become self-critical. The antidote to your feeling less helpless and stuck is, I believe, taking action, doing something different, without getting bogged down worrying so much about doing it right. I'd like to help you not be so hard on yourself and support you in making some behavioral changes.

Does this make sense to you?

The reason we are encouraging each of these clients to reach out toward others is because in contrast to anxiety and anger, depression clearly thrives on isolation, and simply being around others helps counter the depressive state of mind. We also encourage their seeking outside supports so that as clinicians we do not inadvertently become the client's primary source of support. We can imagine that Harold and Abby would feel better talking in therapy. They have a place and relationship to express their emotions and gain the ongoing support that is in such short supply in their daily lives. But we are creating dependency, a serious clinical and ethical issue. Rather than coming to rely on us, they need to approach their anxiety and develop the skills to create their own networks of support.

Karen, of course, isn't immune to this, and in fact the dangers of transference are increased. Given the lack of support and loneliness in her marriage, these needs could easily be shifted to a therapist. The transference may be stronger for a male, but it is more the intimacy of therapy that would be most seductive. If she allowed herself to lean into the relationship she would feel better, and we would feel that the therapy is working because she is, but again it is because we've helped create a dependency.

This is another case in which we need to be clear with ourselves as quickly as possible about what we don't want to do. We know we need to be attentive so that we do not potentially replicate and trigger in her mind her husband's behavior, but we also need to be alert so that we don't allow ourselves to essentially take on the role of ideal spouse. And so we need to encourage her to reach out to others for support and reach out to her husband to help him understand what she needs and begin to create intimacy.

While we are obviously contouring our treatment plans to each client's particular situation, the primary goals of recognizing the depressed mind, taking action, behaviorally solving problems, and focusing on core dynamics exist in each. Again, we present our plan and look for agreement before assigning homework.

ASSIGNING HOMEWORK

As in anxiety and anger, a good starting point is asking clients to be aware of their depressed state of mind—times when they worry about the future, are self-critical, and feel trapped and that nothing will change or that any efforts will be for naught—and label it. We can then suggest first aid techniques—engaging in a mindful activity, writing down how they are feeling, deciding if there is a concrete problem that they need to address—stressing that this stepping back will actually help them rewire their brains and feel more in control. Finally we can begin to work on core dynamics—asking Harold, for example, to note when he feels irritable and to ask himself what else he might be feeling, or asking

Karen to particularly notice when her critical voice discourages her from doing something she wants.

We can also assign some small new concrete behaviors: Harold can make an appointment to talk with his wife's doctor or discuss with his son help with caring for his mother; Abby can make concrete plans even there in the session for what she might do over the weekend, can have reading assignments on adjustment to divorce, or even do the letter-writing exercise; Karen can talk to her husband about coming in for therapy and asking if he would be willing to come in with her for a session, or she can invite someone after church to have lunch with her. We don't want to overload clients with assignments but rather offer options so we can negotiate what is truly an acceptable risk that each is willing to attempt. Our aim is to send the message that treatment and change begins now.

SECOND SESSION

In our treatment maps for anxiety and anger we made first aid techniques and self-regulation the priority of the opening sessions. While we may need to do the same with clients like Harold where there is agitation and anger, our overall approach to depression is looser and more flexible, with our focus on concrete problem solving and upgrading coping skills. In this second session we have several options. Certainly we want to follow up on homework: Harold's call to the doctor and his results in noticing other emotions, Abby's reaction to her reading or letter writing, Karen's discussion with her husband or lunch date—and ask all about their abilities to notice, label, and behaviorally override their depressed state of mind. We need to decide what we can successfully accomplish within the session time.

So we may spend this session teaching Harold meditation and EFT or ask him more about how he explains to himself the changes in his life or about losses in his past as a way of further exploring his grief and tapping into underlying softer emotions. If Abby has completed her letters the remainder of the session will be focused on that, and if not, we may start with the deconstruction of her relationship, asking how she coped with her husband's criticism and explained it to herself when it occurred. If Karen's husband agreed to come to the next session, we may spend the time mapping out with Karen what it is she most wants him to understand and how we can be of support during the process, or we can ask about interests and passions she enjoyed in the past that she can explore now or discuss concrete means, such as volunteering, that can get her out of the house and around others.

As with other aspects of the Boot Camp approach, we are clearly leading but not pulling. We are raising problems that need to be solved, exploring emotions that need to be resolved and patterns that need to be changed. We are moving toward the holes, always checking that the client is in step with us and, if not, explaining our thinking—how our questions and topics are linked to the client's presenting concerns.

BRINGING IN OTHERS

We discussed bringing in friends and family as part of the other treatment maps because these others can often be a support as well as part of the problem that needs to be solved. This is true with depression and probably more so because, as mentioned, there is the need to counter the fueling effects of isolation and offset the trapped feeling through action. Others can also give us a more realistic picture of the client's life situation that we then can use as "reality checks" in future sessions. If Harold's wife, for example, was physically able to attend a session meeting we would have a clearer sense of what Harold actually has to struggle with on a daily basis, as well as an opportunity for them both to talk about the impact of changes on them as a couple. Similarly, if Harold were to invite his son in, we could hear directly from him what he can and cannot do to help his father, rather than relying on what Harold, in his depressed state of mind, imagines his son's response would be.

If Abby's husband were willing to join Abby for a session, at the outset we would need to make clear what the goal is—to give them an opportunity to better understand each other's perspectives and have a more complete picture of the relationship—rather than the session being any semblance of couple therapy, and certainly not a forum for opening old wounds. To avoid falling into these potholes, we need to lead the process and keep a firm hand on what unfolds. The best way to do this is to essentially have each do a monologue shaped by the questions we ask. We needn't be afraid to ask hard questions. We may ask her husband, "What Abby describes as your being critical of her, how do you see it? What is it that you feel Abby doesn't understand about you most?"—and we want to stop any attempts by either of them to play courtroom by stacking up evidence and angrily defending their case. We want instead to focus on soft emotions, move the conversation toward a deeper self-reflection. Ideally we are looking for ways to share emotions—how each felt unappreciated, for example—even though they expressed these feelings differently. Because couple sessions are all about balance, we want to make sure that by the end each partner has had a chance to be heard, and that both walk out with a different perspective and story, however slight.

A session with Karen and her husband would obviously take a different course, since we are de facto doing a modified form of couples therapy, albeit for the one session. Through choreographing this session with Karen in the prior one, we know how to steer the conversation, and she, being prepared, can take the risk of being more honest and assertive. As with Abby and her husband, we want to make sure that Karen's husband, as the "outsider" of the therapeutic relationship, doesn't feel ganged up on by Karen and us. If Karen talks about feeling lonely, for example, and wishing she and her husband could do more together, we want him to be able to express not only his own feelings about the relationship but also his own vision.

Our focus once again is on process rather than content. We

need to resist any pressure we may feel to help them come up with compromises or solutions and instead focus on the problem-solving process in the room—the ability to be honest, to be heard, to not get stuck in defensiveness or fall back into withdrawal. By the end of the session we would hope that both Karen and her husband felt the session was helpful, that the emotional climate had changed, that they better understood how the other felt and had a willingness to continue talking and working on changing the patterns.

One of the ways of working may be that they begin couples therapy, and this becomes a fork in the road in our treatment with Karen. If they want to meet once more as a couple to iron out a plan for behavioral change, follow up on a plan they have created, or even have occasional and widely spaced check-in sessions, that's fine. But as mentioned in Chapter 4, moving into ongoing couples work is something else entirely. Not only does this potentially derail the individual goals of Karen's treatment plan—for example, expanding her social network or reducing her voices of self-criticism—but it also unbalances the system by making her too much the identified patient. Doing so will only reinforce any notions her husband may have that she is the one who really has the problems.

So we need to have a conversation with Karen about clinical options because she is our primary client; we need to discuss what her priorities are, what goals she feels she is able to focus on. If she feels that an intensive effort at couples work is really what she needs to change the quality of her life and relieve her depression, we can support her decision and refer her to another therapist. If she and her husband want to try changing patterns on their own, we can support that as well and use our individual sessions with her to help her stay assertive and clear while she works simultaneously on other behavioral goals. Because the primary focus in treating depression is action and problem solving, where she decides to direct her efforts is less important than the fact that she is doing something concrete and different. The action, once again, is the antidote.

FURTHER SESSIONS

And action will be our focus for future sessions whether the action be environmental, as in taking social risks and being assertive with others, or internal, as in recognizing and behaviorally countering the depressed state of mind and self-criticism, increasing the emotional range, or understanding childhood coping styles and moving toward the adult state. Once we have loosened the hold of grief through our exploration and use of experiential techniques, once clients begin to shift from a reactive to a proactive stance and are clear about where they need to focus, we can begin to spread out sessions and use them for check-ins, fine-tuning, and accountability.

Morita was right. If we help clients create a daily life that better represents who they are and what they need, so they can actively solve the problems that stand in their way, their emotions will in fact catch up. This is a message of hope that we believe and restate over and over when on bad days clients feel discouraged or overwhelmed. We use the sessions to refocus and regroup, and we may make the steps a little smaller to ensure success, but we encourage clients not to fall back into standing still and being stuck.

MEDICATION AGAIN

As mentioned, medication can be helpful in breaking the depressive cycle and in jump-starting change. For those who have not been on medication before, it can help them see that there are in fact biochemical aspects to depression rather than depression being the result of personality defects, as their depressive mind tells them. It can ignite a sense of hope as they feel their moods change. For clients who have taken medication in the past and felt it didn't work or that they couldn't tolerate the side effects, we can say that there are always new medications becoming available that may work more effectively, or that a consultation with a psychiatrist familiar with different options may be a better route than relying on a family doctor.

Medication can also help make therapy more effective. As clients have more energy or are less self-critical, they are better able to hear and understand what we are suggesting and are more inclined to move forward and take risks. Some clients, of course, will feel better on medication and will stop therapy, using the medication to better adjust to dysfunctional patterns instead of grabbing the opportunity to change them. Others, uncomfortable with side effects or the feeling of being dependent on a pill, will go off the medication quickly. We will then need to see how well they can move ahead with our encouragement and outside supports. As with anxiety and anger, our approach toward depression is always pragmatic and lies in our willingness and ability to be creative and change oriented.

This completes our discussion of the Boot Camp approach to depression. Again, by way of summary, here is the treatment map for depression:

Treatment Map For Depression

OVERALL TREATMENT GOALS AND TASKS
- Recognize the depressed state of mind
- Take control; stop feeling trapped—calm depressed mind; take action toward solving problems
- Increase emotional flexibility; act on strong emotions
- Link to personality: Counter critical voice; move toward wants rather than shoulds; learn to act in spite of emotions; resolve grief; move toward adult

SESSION 1 • GOALS AND TASKS
- Assess: type of depression (situational, grief, biological); awareness of state of mind; triggers; ability to override emotion/critical voice; awareness of anger; medication; personal/family history

- Change emotional climate (focus on soft emotions, education, leadership, listening and support)
- Link problem to personality (show relationship triangle; identify rescuer/victim/persecutor roles vs. adult)
- Educate: depression as feeling trapped; need to recognize state of mind; need to act to override emotion; need to override critical voice; understand process of grief
- Present treatment plan: taking concrete action; resolving grief
- Get on same page (track process like a bloodhound)—making sure client understands link between plan and depression
- Assign homework: awareness of depressed mind; triggers; letter writing; concrete behavioral action

SESSION 2 • GOALS AND TASKS

- Feedback on homework
- Depression: Teach meditation; awareness of self-criticism; identify and use anger as information; define wants; develop problem-solving steps
- Plan agenda for family/friend session if applicable

SESSION 3 • GOALS AND TASKS

- Feedback on homework
- Family/friends: Discuss how to support with depression; deconstruct lost relationships; solve concrete relationship problems
- Fine-tune treatment plan: Determine where clients are stuck—assignments too big, need to develop skills, need medication to break cycle, something else?—explore

FURTHER SESSIONS

- Assign behavioral homework
- Focus on behaviorally moving toward action, overriding

critical voice, concrete ways of solving problems and feeling less trapped
- Accountability—use sessions to help clients stay on track
- Determine what additional supports are needed for success

In the next, and last, chapter, we will explore ways of integrating the approach into your own therapeutic style.

CHAPTER SIX

Integrating the Boot Camp Approach Into Your Own Therapeutic Style

SO MAYBE YOU ARE THINKING that you want to apply the Boot Camp approach to some of your cases. Maybe you are interested in increasing your clinical repertoire, or you're working in a setting where there is a waiting list or pressure to do more short-term work, or you're dealing with clients or insurance companies that are limiting the number of allowable sessions. Whatever your reason, the challenge of learning any new clinical approach is making it your own. In this chapter we will look at ways of integrating it into your clinical practice. There are three ways of doing this. One way is to apply the session-by-session treatment maps to selected clients from beginning to end—a "whole case" approach. Another way—an à la carte approach—is to choose concepts, techniques, and models that most appeal to you, ones that you can experiment with and gradually incorporate into your work. Finally, you can create some combination of these two choices. Regardless of your clinical style and orientation, the goal here, to quote Goldilocks, is to help you create the mix that is "just right."

Shifting Gears

But before we do that, let's talk about the challenges of moving from a longer-term model to one that is brief. If this is new to you, such a clinical shift can seem a bit disorienting and even uncomfortable in a couple of ways. One is that you are likely to feel that what you are doing is incomplete in both assessment and treatment. If, for example, you are used to a more detailed assessment process occurring over several sessions, the quick-march assessment of a first session can leave you worrying that you are missing something important. If your model is more psychodynamic, focused on peeling away layers of the past and centered around the transference and countertransference aspects of the therapeutic relationship, or if your model is simply more long term, providing steady support as clients negotiate the challenges of their lives, the shorter-seeming time frame and more narrow focus can cause you to feel there is much potentially left undone.

And then there is the process and pace of brief therapy itself: This type of therapy, with its directive stance, moving quickly to treatment and behavioral change, is more of a sprint than a marathon. It's easy to feel that your leadership in fact borders on being controlling, or that your pacing is off, that you are pushing clients before they are ready, or that you are not giving them the time and opportunity to define their own path or develop their own insights. Most of all you will be rushed, as though you were pushing yourself to play a piece on the piano at a faster tempo than you feel capable of producing. You may get through it but not be aware of what you just did.

All this is to be expected, since you are stepping outside your comfort zone. But like the piano playing you will undoubtedly find that it all turns out better than it feels, that what you fear might happen does not, and that with practice the initially frantic pace will become your new normal. By setting expectations with clients at the initial contact and by getting ongoing feedback through tracking the process tightly, your worry that you are dragging the client along will dissipate; your feeling rattled by having an incomplete assessment before beginning treatment will abate when you see that there are indeed plenty of opportunities to adjust your impressions as you get feedback from clients and fine-tune their treatment. Rather than being two separate processes, assessment and treatment in brief therapy actually form a circular path, with each fueling the other.

Boot-Camping Clients: Whole-Case Guidelines

If you have had some experience with doing brief therapy, either by choice or because of job requirements, the Boot Camp approach can offer you variations on the theme and help you expand your perspective and skills. If you are trained to do long-term work, you can think of applying the Boot Camp approach to one or two cases at a time as being similar to taking a mini-language-immersion course. You may feel unsettled a good part of the time, not completely clear about where you are headed, but if you follow the program, you may be surprised at the end by how much you have learned. Here are some guidelines to consider before stepping out:

Choose appropriate clients. A psychiatric social worker at the local hospital is doing discharge for Ms. Harris, a patient who came in for a several-day stay following a suicide attempt by overdose. The social worker informs you that while Ms. Harris is currently on medication, she has a history of being inconsistent and that she has no family in the area and few friends. Finally, the patient began struggling with severe job stress after the company she worked for was sold to a different firm, and this stress, in fact, is what precipitated the attempt. Is the Boot Camp approach a good idea for this patient? Not really.

While the patient may benefit from behavioral interventions, the fact that she is marginally stable, has few outside supports, may or may not stay on medication, and is struggling with job stress over which she undoubtedly has limited control makes her clinically inappropriate for the approach. She will need ongoing support until you are clear she is no longer so fragile and has the resources to manage her stress and depression.

As mentioned in the opening chapter of this book, brief work should not be used with clients who need the longer-term support of a therapeutic relationship, whether because of their own isolation, their limited skills or learning abilities, or the fragility of their mental state. It can be effective with those who are relatively stable, even if struggling, and who have internal and external resources. While you don't need to compromise your strengths and style, you have a responsibility to discern what might work best with clients and continually assess along the way whether the model is a good fit. This is part of your leadership and professionalism. If in doubt, seek consultation with a colleague.

Avoid radical shifts. You have been working with Jack and his depression for several months using an insight-oriented approach, but you're feeling stuck. While he seems to have occasional "Aha" moments and is much more aware of the origin of his coping style, his overall level of depression isn't really much better. You're thinking that maybe a change of approach is what is needed and that the Boot Camp approach, with its behavioral aspects, may help him dig out emotionally.

Don't attempt this approach. While you may want to experiment with incorporating behavioral assignments into the therapy, you also want to avoid the radical shift of tossing out your overall approach. This is too disorienting for clients and too easily misinterpreted. Given his state of mind, we can easily imagine Jack's feeling that it is his fault that things aren't better, or that you are giving up and trying to push him out the door. Furthermore, there's a good chance this isn't about Jack but about you and your frustration. The problem in the room is the stuckness, and the stuckness is a symptom of an underlying problem. This is what you need to get on the table and explore with Jack, to help him understand your thinking. If there is a sincere agreement that a change in focus is called for, then slowly begin to integrate it into your treatment plan or refer him to a different therapist.

Map out the treatment plan in advance. While pragmatism and flexibility are at the heart of the Boot Camp approach, it's useful to think through your goals and tasks session by session for the first several sessions. Map out for yourself, for example, what you need to cover in the first session so you can stay focused and move the process along. Since you know what the presenting problem is from your initial contact, think through your assessment questions and the homework assignments you may give. This type of preparation not only will help you reduce your own anxiety but also will help you more clearly map out the terrain for clients, which, in turn, will help you stay on target.

Try to stay within time limits. Having a map for sessions can help you stay focused and active within the session, but you will undoubtedly feel rushed if your style is less directive. Again, while the session process is not a forced march, and you want to build rapport and make certain that clients stay in step with you, you may need to push yourself a bit to accomplish what you set out to do at the beginning of the session. It's back to the piano playing—feeling awkward at first, but finding it easier to move along as your skills become honed. Pushing yourself to stay within time limits will also help you to avoid inadvertently sliding back into your old style and approach.

Be easy on yourself. A parallel process unfolds as you apply the Boot Camp approach to specific cases. Just as you want to encourage and support clients in taking acceptable risks and breaking out of old patterns, you also want to do this for yourself. The key here, as it is with clients, is doing it differently rather than doing it right. You want to adopt an attitude of experimentation and even playfulness. There are no mistakes, just the learning of new skills. Pat yourself on the back for your efforts, just as you would do with clients.

Developing and Integrating Boot Camp Skills

If you are interested in experimenting with various elements of the Boot Camp approach, either to incorporate them into your existing clinical models or so that you can step more slowly into the Boot Camp waters, here is an à la carte menu. Items are clustered into various types of process skills, tools and techniques, and concepts with guidelines on ways to learn and integrate skills into your everyday practice. Some of these ideas repeat foundational concepts defined in Chapters 1 and 2, but I present them again here as menu items, of sorts, to help you pick and choose which will work best for you.

PROCESS SKILLS

Because process is at the heart of the Boot Camp approach and of therapy, these skills have wide applicability to most clinical approaches.

Tracking the process like a bloodhound. Because we have focused on this skill so much, it seems appropriate that we start here with the ability to closely track the process within the session. The main obstacle to doing this is a tendency to get lost in the content of the client's story. We either get fascinated by the story itself or, like a detective, hang on to a client's every word, connecting dots, looking for gaps, and instinctively starting to put together the puzzle pieces of the client's historical and situational landscape. Obviously you need to be able to do this to some extent, but you don't want to get so caught up in this that you are overlooking what is happening there in the room, particularly nonverbal behaviors. If you feel you are weak in these skills, there are a couple of things you can do to ramp up your awareness.

One is just to practice focusing on the nonverbal process in conversations in general. When you watch a movie, turn down the sound and watch facial expressions; when you see couples talking in a restaurant, see if you can tell whether they are in sync; when engaged in a casual conversation yourself, try focusing on the nonverbal interactions rather than exclusively on the story, and see what you notice.

The close tracking becomes essential at those critical break points within a session when you offer an interpretation, provide education, or explain your treatment plan. What is easy to do when hearing any negative reaction is to try to make your point stronger—repeating what you just said, adding more information, and so on. Rather than try to override with more content, deal with the process, the negativity itself. The mindset here is to say what you are going to say and then take a breath and stop. Watch carefully what happens next. Look for agreement. If it is not there, back up, question the reason for the hesitation, and then address and clarify.

A good way to become more sensitive to these break points without the pressure of thinking on your feet is to watch videotapes of yourself or other clinicians, or even listen to audiotapes, looking for agreement, hesitations, or "yes, buts" following a clinician's comment. These are invaluable in training your eyes and ears to catch when clients are falling out of step.

Showing leadership and the active role. Tracking the process is a matter of developing a focus and attuning your listening and observational skills. Shifting to a highly interactive role in the session is, as mentioned earlier, usually more difficult because you simply feel uncomfortable with a more active format. The key here is not worrying so much about content and what to say next and when—having a map for the session will help you stay on course—but rather to allow yourself to be more spontaneous, less cautious.

Not getting lost in the content will certainly help give you the mental space to do this. But the other element is to take the risk of saying what comes to your mind rather than self-censoring or deliberating about timing and correctness. This can feel a bit like doing a trapeze act without a net if this is not your style, but it helps to remember that you are using behavioral change rather than insight as your primary tool. And if you are tracking the process closely, if what you say confuses the client or creates some resistance right there in the room, you will be able to catch it and repair it.

That said, you don't want to dominate the conversation. You

are leading and guiding, not pulling. If a client shuts down or begins to glaze over, you'll know that you're talking too much; the client is getting flooded. Stop, check in with the client—"I realize that I was just giving you a lot of information at one time. What are you thinking?"—and see what happens next.

A good way of increasing your spontaneity in sessions is to practice outside them with family and friends. Pay some attention to yourself when you are talking with others; notice ideas and images as they pop up in your mind. Rather than going on autopilot, letting the other shape the conversation, holding back, or worrying about what the other person may think, try speaking up and saying what is on your mind as it unfolds. If you feel a bit anxious when doing this, it is a good indicator that you are stepping outside your style and plowing new ground. Do it, see what happens, and pat yourself on the back for the effort. Then try doing the same in sessions.

Working within session time limits. If you want to learn to manage the time within a session more efficiently, you need to begin by clearly mapping in advance the material you want to cover. Many of us already rely on some mental format for first sessions, and in certain work settings the first-session material, such as completing intake, HIPPA, or clinical assessment forms, is prescribed. In the Boot Camp approach, as mentioned in earlier chapters, we have basically four goals for the first session: changing the emotional climate, linking problems to personality by identifying the core dynamic, presenting a clear treatment plan, and making certain the client is in step with us by tracking the process all along the way. By setting a goal to cover this material by the end of the session, you can train yourself to become more proactive, structured, and efficient.

Think again about our physician analogy. What our physician does in 15 minutes we want to do in 50. It is helpful to think of the session as composed of segments—opening, exploration, education, treatment plan, homework—and to proceed through these segments, watching the clock as you do so. Avoid getting lost in the story and content, and while you do want to tap into soft emotions, be careful not to intentionally pursue potentially emotion-laden topics such as trauma or abuse. Not only will stirring up discussion of such events potentially derail the session process, but more concerning, it may derail the clinical relationship. Uncovering too much sensitive emotional material in the first session can leave the new client feeling overwhelmed, ungrounded, and unsafe. The Boot Camp approach manages this by moving quickly through assessment material; that said, if a client does unexpectedly get emotionally overwhelmed—if Harold, for example, begins to break down and sob about his wife—our agenda goes out the window. We should do our best to support him and then follow up to make certain that he is not, in fact, left overwhelmed or frightened by his outpouring of emotion.

The mapping and time management that you do for the first session can easily be applied to subsequent sessions, even if you decide to use a treatment map different from the Boot Camp's. If you are able to take a proactive stance, let clients know at the start that your work together is a partnership with both of you taking responsibility for working toward goals and setting a session's agenda; and act as the leader, process watcher, and timekeeper, you can make sure that the session stays close to its agenda. By doing this, you are being a role model for clients—they can take that same role in actively pursuing their goals in their everyday lives.

Avoiding rewounding. This is both a concept and process issue. By rewounding we are talking about not replicating past dysfunctional patterns and roles in the therapeutic relationship. It is a concept that is part of our countertransference and according to the Boot Camp approach a source of client resistance; it is a process issue because we need to be highly alert to potential rewounding in the session process.

This knowing what we don't want to do is relatively easy to determine if we are alert to it. As mentioned in Chapter 5, Abby's description of her "critical" husband, for example, tells us about her heightened sensitivity to perceptions of criticism, as well as a certain tolerance for it, undoubtedly evidence of an old child-hood wound. We need to mentally note this and continually look for verbal or nonverbal signs in the session process that she has been inadvertently triggered. If we miss these, and replicate the relationship problem and process, she will eventually leave us the same way she left her husband.

The skill here is detecting this as quickly as possible. Even in the initial phone contact, listen for client complaints about others. Ask in the first session about past therapy experiences and listen to how the client describes the therapist. Ask about break points in past relationships, when clients have left, after reaching some emotional bottom line. The goal isn't necessarily to deconstruct each and every one of these past experiences, but rather to identify and behaviorally change the response to present triggers.

Making quick assessments. This brings us to the related skill of making quick assessments and yet another potential source of initial discomfort. While the Boot Camp approach draws heavily on the relationship triangle and core dynamic as a focus for assessments, any clinical model and map that is clear and able to help you confirm or deny your initial hypotheses about a client's problem and solution will work. What is important is that the assessment be concise, that you once again thwart any temptations to get bogged down in backstory and content. Think of the physician with her pointed questions about symptoms and what has been tried, her checklist of family history.

Don't be reckless; take the time you need to assess Ms. Harris (the patient mentioned earlier) and her resources, trust your instincts, and obviously don't rationalize to yourself that she is able to do what someone more emotionally stable can do. But also don't rationalize that every client requires the same degree of thoroughness because it fits within your own comfort zone. You can backfill with more details and history if and when clients get emotionally or behaviorally stuck in making progress. Experiment with moving ahead at a quicker pace than you may be used to even if you feel less than certain and comfortable.

TECHNIQUES AND TOOLS

Many of the techniques and tools described in our treatment maps are probably, in some form, already in your repertoire. But if there are some you want to add, here is a list of the major ones, along with tips for learning and incorporating them:

Changing the emotional climate. We all hope clients will feel better after the first session than they did at the start, but this becomes a goal in and of itself in the Boot Camp approach and other brief models. Don't get lost in content, notice the nonverbal indicators of especially soft emotions, and don't be afraid to stop the storytelling to explore them.

Noticing and acting are the first steps; then comes mentally choreographing your next move. Some clinicians miss opportunities for changing the emotional climate, not because they fail to notice the process, but because they fail to use the full power of their voice. Your voice is another tool in your clinical toolbox, and some therapists get so caught up in focusing on what they want to say that they pay little attention to how they say it. You want to be conscious of and deliberate about how you sound, especially when confronting emotions, and the general rule is to mirror the clients' emotions and sounds—by sounding quiet and reflective when they are, for example, and matching them should their moods shift.

That said, you always keep in mind any danger of triggering rewounding; you want to convey safety and concern and when unsure, be gentle in order to tunnel under clients' defenses rather than strengthening them by inadvertently raising fear and anxiety. Like the other skills, this use of voice is a matter of practice. Recording your sessions can help you become sensitive to how you sound, as can listening to and observing other clinicians.

Using the ideal voice. These voice skills become particularly important if you decide to use the ideal voice technique. Essentially you are acting out the part of the ideal other, and for the technique to have the full impact it is important to convey the emotion—the husband's regret, the supervisor's confusion—as well as the words.

To map this out in your mind, visualize what your client would most need to hear to feel understood and healed. Preface the statements with "What if . . . came to you and said. . . ." Be honest, talk about intentions, and use a gentle voice: "I just want to let you know I am sorry for . . . I acted the way I did (or said what I said) because I was worried about . . . I would like us to be able to. . . ." At first you will probably need to plan these statements in advance, but with experience you will be able to use the technique spontaneously in a session.

Using education. Naming, normalizing, and defining problems help put clients' distorted thinking and anxiety to rest. Successfully incorporating education into your sessions, especially the first session, is a matter of managing the time within the sessions and knowing what you want to say. Don't put pressure on yourself to wing it; instead develop 5-minute speeches on depression, anxiety, and anger that fit into your clinical model.

Talking about genetics, brain functioning, and the limited ways children have to cope with their world helps counter clients' own assault on their personality and inadequacy. Describing brain rewiring, upgrading coping skills, and talking about increasing flexibility steers thinking away from the concept of right and wrong. End your speech on implications for treatment: "So even though you learned to be hypervigilant and walk on eggshells around others, it would be good if you now could learn to be more assertive, more adult, and less fearful; this is something we can work on together."

Using the relationship triangle. The relationship triangle is clearly a concept, one that is helpful for quick assessment (roles and personalities) and treatment planning (becoming adult), but it is also a tool that you can use as a supplement to your own approach. Its strengths are that it is visual and normalizing (this is what people in relationships often do or how people prone to depression and anxiety often think) and helps explain to clients, without judgment, angry outbursts, acting out, anxiety, depression, self-criticism, low self-esteem, and the process of couples struggling and even veering toward divorce. You can present it as "Here is another way of looking at . . . [whatever you have just explained]."

Learn and practice the description presented in Chapter 2. Leave about 10 minutes in a session to explain it and get client feedback. It is helpful to individualize your examples and echo client information and language as much as possible to help clients apply it. For example, if a client talks about "doing a lot and feeling unappreciated," use those same words when describing the rescuer. If someone tends to act out by binge eating, say that when folks feel resentful and move to the persecutor role they may act out by suddenly exploding or having affairs or going on an eating binge. And, you say, they feel like they deserve to do it—explaining, normalizing, and reframing the behavior—to counter their own thoughts that their behavior is seemingly uncontrollable and irrational. Finally, emphasize the qualities and differences of the adult so clients clearly understand the healthier alternative that you are presenting. Once they have the diagram in their minds, you can refer back to "adult" to reinforce the notion of balance and self-differentiation.

Assigning homework. Homework speeds up the treatment process by allowing clients to practice skills outside the office and by making a clear statement to clients that therapy is more than talking about one's life but also involves taking active steps to change it. Make homework assignments clear, concrete, and achievable. First assignments are usually observational—"Notice how you feel when . . ."; "Pay attention to . . ."—with no request for change. These are warm-up exercises, so to speak, to help clients be proactive and to help you see if clients are on board with you and the treatment plan.

But subsequent assignments need to move clients out of their comfort zones into behavioral action, yet at the same time not be too overwhelming. This becomes the challenge—creating a psychological and behavioral stretch that the client can successfully perform. It's helpful to think in terms of applying broad individual skills—assertiveness, for example—in ever more challenging ways, moving up the anxiety hierarchy from strangers to friends or family members, rather than thinking in terms of challenging clients to resolve specific situations and problems (having a client talk to her husband about whether he wants to move to New Mexico or not, for example). While we certainly want to help clients solve concrete problems, try focusing on the point in the process where clients get stuck solving their own problems. Think of the content of their current problems as merely a reflection of this deeper deficiency that they need to attend to.

If, for example, 16-year-old Sam is conditioned to hold his tongue and is unable to tell his mother what is bothering him, causing him to have depression and anxiety, it is better to think of his challenge as approaching his anxiety and being assertive—which is key to upgrading and developing a more flexible coping style—rather than as merely a mother-child relationship issue. His response to his mother is only the current stuck point in his ability to communicate his thoughts and needs. Pressuring him to move toward quickly changing his pattern with his mother not only can potentially replicate the problem (the therapist becomes another adult who seems intimidating) but also can overwhelm him and lead to failure.

Instead, give Sam the assignment of noticing social situations, perhaps talking with friends at school, in which he holds back, and ask him to try to go against the grain and take the risk of saying what he is thinking. If he does that successfully, his next assignment could be doing the same with an low-risk adult—for example, approaching a teacher who harshly graded one of his papers. With each success his self-confidence grows and with your encouragement and support he will be ready to take on his biggest challenge—namely, his mother.

Keep in mind that you can stack assignments so that clients can continue to work on several treatment goals at one time. One week Tanisha may be given an assignment to practice using EFT when she is anxious, the following week to have a conversation with her supervisor about her work schedule and use EFT ahead of time if she is anxious, and the week following that to offset her depressive mindset by writing out daily appreciations before she goes to bed while also following up with her supervisor and using EFT when needed. We are encouraging her to work on both new and old skills, short- and long-term goals. It is when clients don't follow through with an assignment that we need to regroup and determine the problem, for example, that the conversation with the supervisor was too much of a challenge for Tanisha, or she didn't use the EFT because she didn't fully understand how to do it, or she didn't do the appreciations because she didn't see the link between them and her depression.

Employing self-regulation techniques. The various self-regulation techniques for anxiety and anger are always handy tools to have at your disposal to offer clients. Not only does your teaching and assigning them give clients concrete actions to take that help them feel less "victimized" by their emotions, but they reinforce the notion of emotional responsibility and adult behavior. If you want to expand your repertoire, there are numerous texts that offer a catalog of methods that clients can learn quickly and then practice.

One of the advantages of EFT over other "power therapy" techniques, such as eye movement desensitization and reprocessing (EMDR), is that clients can do EFT on their own as needed once they learn the steps, rather than having to work with you in your office. Because it may seem to clients (and you) more complex and esoteric than other self-regulation techniques, and in order to avoid triggering their wariness and anxiety, it is important that you feel comfortable with it yourself before presenting it. The best way to do this is to practice it on yourself or friends and family so you can actually see the results and feel comfortable with the technique. As mentioned earlier, there is much additional information on this on websites and in YouTube videos, as well as in professional texts, such as those by Gallo (2004), and training workshops.

CONCEPTS

Just as working with process and experimenting with techniques can expand what you do within sessions, integrating some of the core concepts or the Boot Camp approach can expand how you think about the problems clients present. Again, here are some guidelines for integrating them into your current models:

Patterns. The Boot Camp approach, like other systems-based models, looks at changing behavioral patterns. The focus is on the interactional rather than the intrapsychic, and the core belief is that the DNA of dysfunction lies in the pattern enacted between two people rather than within the psychology of one person, and that the pattern is always more powerful than the people. This way of describing relationship problems helps offset client self-criticism, and because the initial goal is to simply stop the pattern, clients, particularly those who tend toward perfectionism, feel less pressure to do it right.

If this is a new way of thinking for you, the starting point, like the focus on process, is to increase your awareness through practice. Forget about content; instead look at the tennis match of emotional exchange and nonverbal behaviors. Look at the way two individuals bounce off each other, the A-to-B and B-to-A sequences: Tom asks a question, Ann ignores him, Tom raises his voice, Ann ignores him, Tom yells, Ann screams back, Tom walks away in a huff. Regardless of content—cleaning a room, doing homework—the pattern is the same. Just as you can become more aware of nonverbal interactions by watching couples and families at restaurants or by watching movies, you can do these same things to develop your pattern-detection skills.

To map patterns in sessions with individuals, ask "what happens next" questions: "So you ask your daughter to clean her room, and what happens next? So she says that, and then what do you do?" You want to be able to visualize in your own mind the sequence of actions. Once you identify the sequence, present it to the client and see if it is what the client sees playing out. From there you can talk about the power of patterns in shaping relationships and explain that when one person changes his or her step in the dance, the other person will have to change as well.

Relationship triangle. The relationship triangle is just a specific type of pattern. We described above how it is used as a tool to help clients understand the source of their problem, but obviously the triangle is conceptual as well. To use it as part of your assessment, visualize the triangle, with its roles and dynamic shifts to the persecutor role, as clients or couples talk about their relationships. You can begin to map out roles in broad strokes—those who follow the rules, are nice, and are overresponsible are rescuers; those who become overwhelmed and feel helpless are victims; those who are aggressive and angry are persecutors. Ask questions about the details of the personalities—Does the rescuer ever feel unappreciated or have a difficult time making decisions? Does the victim get flooded with anxiety or feel besieged by problems? Then map out the move to the persecutor—Does the rescuer ever feel resentful that others aren't helping out? Does the victim feel that others are micromanaging him or her at times? Once you can see a tight fit between the triangle model and the client's relationship patterns, present your conclusions to the client to explain and normalize their behaviors.

Being adult. Attorneys talk about the reasonable man defense, in which the question is asked, What would we expect a reasonable man to do in this situation? This is essentially what the adult is about, thinking in terms of what a reasonable adult would do—not emotional, yet assertive; clear but not controlling; responsible but not overresponsible or hypervigilant. Just as it is helpful to ask "What happens next?" questions to map patterns, keep in mind what an adult would do in a given situation and ask, essentially, what kept clients from being adult: "So your boss said you couldn't have the weekend off. Why didn't you say that you had already put in your request 2 months ago, rather than getting angry and stomping out of the office?" Or to a couple: "So you were talking about setting a new bedtime for your son. What caused this to turn into such a huge argument?"

What you are doing by asking these questions is mapping with clients the gap between adult behavior and their response, as well as tracking the patterns that fuel their emotions. You are looking for what they can't do, where they get stuck, what triggers old wounds. What is important when asking such questions is that you sound curious and gentle. You want to make sure that there is no hint of criticism in your voice, no suggestion that clients should simply know better. This will only create resistance and potentially replicate in therapy the problem that clients are experiencing outside of therapy. Once you have mapped this out with clients, show them the relationship triangle, describe the adult, and continue to refer back to it throughout treatment.

Core dynamic. Rather than spending a lot of time tracking down the source and substance of childhood wounds, try skipping the historical focus and instead work toward overriding the impact of these wounds and eventually healing them in the present through behavioral change.

Children have basically three ways of coping—being good, being passive or withdrawn, and being angry. You can use the roles of the relationship triangle to ask pointed questions in your assessment: "Were you a good kid? What did you do when you were afraid of your parents? What are you most sensitive to in others now?" Look once again for what clients are not able to do, that is, the holes, and then encourage them to do the opposite of what they usually do when wounds are triggered—being self-regulating and assertive rather than angry, taking action rather than withdrawing or being passive. Then follow up, tracking where adult behavior has broken down: "So when you were upset at your wife, what kept you from speaking up rather than keeping quiet? What were you most afraid of?" Help clients distinguish past from present, labeling these as different, and assign them homework that both poses an acceptable risk and is likely to have a successful outcome.

States of mind. If you have experience working with traditional cognitive-behavioral approaches, the Boot Camp approach can initially seem reductionistic. But that's the point, not to have clients spend time deconstructing and reconstructing the nuances of their thoughts. Instead help clients simply recognize when anxiety, anger, or depression has taken over so they can take active steps to counter them.

Do this by thinking this way yourself. Think in broad strokes and map these with clients: "So can you tell when your anxious mind is taking over? Can you tell when you are worrying about the future, when you have a hard time reining in your thoughts? Do you notice anything in your body—that gnawing feeling in your stomach or feeling shaky? Can you recognize your depressed state of mind when you have no energy, or feel like nothing matters, or telling yourself that you never do anything right?" Label and move on; avoid content and deconstruction. Write down for clients their own unique symptoms, give this note to them to post somewhere, and assign them the homework of tracking their state of mind several times a day.

Morita therapy. If you are intrigued by the concepts of Morita therapy, you can expand your knowledge by reading about the ToDo Institute on the Internet (www.todoinstitute.org) or David Reynolds's books. But because it is less a set of techniques and more a simple perspective, feel free to experiment with this way of thinking. Try for, say, a week to adopt that state of mind where you override emotions with behavior. When you find yourself ruminating or feeling upset in some way, ask yourself, "What is it that I need to do next?" The answer may be to carry out behavioral action to solve the problem distressing you, or it may be just to move ahead with adult behavior. As with EFT, once you are personally more comfortable with this technique, you can weave it into your clinical practice.

If you are interested in exploring similar and less mainstream clinical approaches, consider neocognitive therapy, also known as psychology of the mind (Mills & Spittle, 2001; Pransky, 2001). Like Morita therapy, this has as its focus overriding emotions with behaviors, but it also incorporates states of mind. Clients learn to recognize the up-and-down natural flow of their daily moods and are taught that when they are in a low mood (or negative state of mind), certain pet peeves (your husband is a slob) or everyday problems (your boss is always critical) will bubble to the surface. Wait, this method says—this is not the time for action because your low mood is clouding your perceptions. Instead, lay low. If you do nothing at all, your mood will improve. Once it rises— when your perspective is naturally more balanced and your creativity is engaged—this is the time to look back at your problems. See what is left, and if problems still exist, now is the time to take steps to solve them.

By experimenting on your own with either or both of these approaches, you can better understand the flow of your emotions and the power of behavior to influence them. This in turn can help you think in these terms with clients, as well as begin to incorporate some of this thinking into your own practice.

WORKING WITH FAMILY AND FRIENDS

Family and friends can be sources of support for clients who are anxious, angry, or depressed, but they are also often implicated in the problems that need to be solved. If you work exclusively with individuals, bringing others into a session may feel a bit disorienting; the intimacy of the one-on-one relationship is broken or at best diluted. Here are some tips for incorporating friends and family into sessions:

Define the goal of the session. Clients will often ask others to come in without giving them any clear idea of the focus. What family and friends are most fearful of is some verbal free-for-all where anything or everything will be dumped on the table, or some dark secret revealed. It's your job to define the goal at the start of session to offset these fears and establish a sense of leadership, which in turn creates safety. This doesn't mean you need to speak for the client, but you want to make clear to everyone what is reasonable to accomplish with the session time: "Margaret and I were talking about ways you might be able to help her when she feels overwhelmed. I'm hoping that we can come up with some concrete steps in this session that you both can try at home."

Take a few minutes to build rapport. Engaging in small talk with friends and family members, for example, about jobs and interests; thanking them for coming in; and checking on how they feel again help them relax and convey safety through your being gently in charge.

Get and keep the conversation going. Your role is that of facilitator, not arbitrator. Ask the client to make an opening statement: "As Kim [the therapist] said, I sometimes feel overwhelmed. Though I know you are trying to be helpful, your getting frustrated with me and taking over doesn't really help me in the long run. I'd like us to do this differently."

Then let them talk. Don't worry about content; instead help them to keep moving forward toward understanding, toward a solution. If they get derailed—Margaret gets emotional or is being unclear—stop and clarify: "Margaret, you are sounding angry; what just happened?" "Margaret, you said that you'd like Joe to just be supportive; what does that mean? How can he show support in a concrete way?"

Make sure the conversation is balanced. You are moving toward a goal; the session is not a place for venting and ranting. Don't be afraid to interrupt; ask one person to stop so the other can talk. Again, you are trying to create a dialogue in which each person's intentions, needs, and behaviors are understood.

Don't be afraid to ask the hard questions. You want to guide the conversation but also take it to a deeper, more honest level. You do this by asking the hard questions, asking about what you think the other may be thinking or feeling: "Joe, Margaret doesn't understand why you get so frustrated. I'm wondering if you ever wish that she could deal with these things on her own rather than always coming to you about them." Joe may say yes or no, but that is not what's important. What is important is stirring the emotional pot, letting both people know that this is the time and place to take the risk of being more open and honest.

Resist the urge to find a solution. As an outsider to the story, you may be able to see the blind spots that the individuals cannot. It's fine to make suggestions—"Have you ever thought of . . . ?"—but be careful that, in order to quell your own anxiety or relieve the tension in the room, you do not step in as the authority or judge. The best solution is the one that clients and their friends and family members can come up with and agree on. It is their ability to talk to one another and work through problems and emotions together—for Margaret to be assertive, for Joe to be able to listen—that over the long haul are what will make their relationships productive and healthy. If there is tension, talk about the tension to dismantle it and get them back on track, rather than jumping to quick solutions.

Take care of yourself. If a client feels it would be good for the entire family to come in at some point, it is up to you to decide whether this is a clinical challenge that you are willing to take or whether, in fact, it is too overwhelming for you. If it is too overwhelming, either bring in a co-therapist to help you manage, or divide the family into subgroups. Don't get hung up on means, but rather focus on ends. Give yourself the time and space you need to build up both your skills and your confidence.

Finis

This concludes our tips for integrating the elements of the Boot Camp approach into your own practice. This also concludes our journey together. It is hoped that these concepts and skills, this way of thinking about the problems of anxiety, anger, and depression, have sparked a renewed reflection of your own assumptions, habits, and methods of practice and have stirred your own creativity. This perhaps is the ultimate purpose of approaching anything new—to shake up the ordinary, to ignite questioning, to stimulate new ideas, and to encourage us to experiment with something that we had not attempted before. This is how we, and by extension our clients, grow. This is how we can help our clients discover who they are, what they believe, and what they need to do most.

Thank you for coming along.

References

Andrews, P., & Thompson, J. (2009). The bright side of being blue: Depression as an adaption for analyzing complex problems. *Psychological Review, 116*(3), 620–654.

Berg, I. (1994). *Family based services: A solution-based approach.* New York: W. W. Norton.

Berg, I., & Steiner, T. (2003). *Children's solution work.* New York: W. W. Norton.

Binder, J. (2010). *Key competencies in brief dynamic psychotherapy.* New York: Guilford.

Bowen, M. (1978). *Family therapy in clinical practice.* New York: Jason Aronson.

Budman, S., Hoyt, M., & Friedman, S., eds. (1992). *First sessions in brief therapy.* New York: Guilford.

Child Welfare Information Gateway. (2009). *Understanding the effects of maltreatment on brain development.* Retrieved January, 30, 2013, from http.www.childwelfare.gov

Cooper, G. (2011). New perspectives on termination. *Psychotherapy Networker, 35*(5), 10–11.

de Shazer, S. (1985). *Keys to solution in brief therapy.* New York: W. W. Norton.

Dimidjian, S., Hollon, S., & Dobson, K. (2006). Randomized trial of behavioral activation, cognitive therapy, and antidepressant medication in the acute treatment of adults with major depression. *Journal of Consulting and Clinical Psychology, 74*(4), 658–670.

Ekstein, R., & Wallerstein, R. (1958). *The teaching and learning of psychotherapy.* New York: Basic Books.

Gallo, F. (2004). *Energy psychology.* (2nd ed.). Boca Raton, FL: CRC Press.

Garfield, S. (1986). Research on client variables in psychotherapy. In S. Garfield & A. Bergin (Eds.), *Handbook of psychotherapy and behavior change* (3rd ed.), pp. 213–256. New York: Wiley.

Gilbert, R., & Gilbert, R. (1992). *Extraordinary relationships: A new way of thinking about human interactions.* New York: Wiley.

Halford, W. (2001). *Brief therapy for couples: Helping partners help themselves.* New York: Guilford.

Hendrix, H. (2007). *Getting the love you want.* New York: Henry Holt.

Karpman, S. (1968). Fairy tales and script drama analysis. *Transactional Analysis Bulletin, 7*(26), 39–43. Retrieved January 30, 2013, from http://www.karpmandramatriangle.com

Kessler, R., Chiu, W., Demler, O., & Walters, E. (2005). Prevalence, severity, and comorbidity of twelve-month DSM-IV disorders in the National Comorbidity Survey Replication (NCS-R). *Archives of General Psychiatry, 62*(6), 617–627.

Klipper, M. Z., & Benson, H. (2000). *The relaxation response.* New York: William Morrow Paperbacks.

Lambert, M., & Bailey, D. (2001). Research summary on the therapeutic relationship and psychotherapy outcome. *Psychotherapy Therapy: Research, Practice, and Training, 38*(4), 357–361.

Lipchik, E. (2002). *Beyond techniques in solution-focused therapy.* New York: Guilford.

Messer, S., & Warren, C. (1998). *Models of brief psychodynamic therapy: A comparative approach.* New York: Guilford.

Mills, R., & Spittle, E. (2001). *The wisdom within.* Renton, WA: Lone Pine.

O'Hanlon, B. (1999). *Do one thing different: Ten simple ways to change your life.* New York: W. W. Norton.

O'Hanlon, B. (2006). *Change 101: Practical guide for creating change in life or therapy.* New York: W. W. Norton.

O'Hanlon, B., & Weiner-Davis, M. (2003). *In search of solutions: A new direction in psychotherapy.* New York: W. W. Norton.

Phillips, E. (1985). *Psychotherapy revised: New frontiers in research and practice.* Hillsdale, NJ: Erlbaum.

Pransky, G. (2001). *The relationship handbook.* La Conner, WA: Pransky & Associates.

Preston, J. (1998). *Integrative brief therapy: Cognitive, psychodynamic, humanistic, and neurobehavioral approaches.* San Luis, CA: Impact.

Renick, O. (2011, July 25). France, U.S. have highest depression rates in world, study suggests. Retrieved January 30, 2013, from http:www.bloomberg.com

Reynolds, D. (1984). *Constructive living.* Honolulu: University of Hawaii Press.

Reynolds, D. (2002). *Handbook for constructive living.* Honolulu: University of Hawaii Press.

Siegel, R. (2011). West meets East. *Psychotherapy Networker, 35*(5), 20–27.

Szabo, P., Meier, D., & Pierolf, K. (2009). *Coaching plain and simple: Solution-focused brief coaching essentials.* New York: W. W. Norton.

Wehrenberg, M. (2008). *The 10 best-ever anxiety management techniques: Understanding how your brain makes you anxious and what you can do to change it.* New York: W. W. Norton.

Weil, A. (2013). *Spontaneous happiness: A new path to emotional well-being.* New York: Little, Brown.

Index